University-Industry Research Interactions

The Technology Policy and Economic Growth Series

Herbert I. Fusfeld and Richard R. Nelson, Editors

Fusfeld/Haklisch INDUSTRIAL PRODUCTIVITY AND
INTERNATIONAL TECHNICAL COOPERATION
Fusfeld/Langlois UNDERSTANDING R&D PRODUCTIVITY
Hazewindus THE U.S. MICROELECTRONICS INDUSTRY:
Technical Change, Industry Growth, and Social Impact
Nelson GOVERNMENT AND TECHNICAL PROGRESS:
A Cross-Industry Analysis

Pergamon Titles of Related Interest

Dewar INDUSTRY VITALIZATION: Toward a
National Industrial Policy
Lundstedt/Colglazier MANAGING INNOVATION: The Social
Dimensions of Creativity, Invention, and Technology

Related Journals*

COMPUTERS AND INDUSTRIAL ENGINEERING
COMPUTERS AND OPERATIONS RESEARCH
SOCIO-ECONOMIC PLANNING SCIENCES
TECHNOLOGY IN SOCIETY

*Free specimen copies available upon request.

University-Industry Research Interactions

edited by
Herbert I. Fusfeld and
Carmela S. Haklisch
*Center for Science
and Technology Policy,
New York University*

The Technology Policy and Economic Growth Series,
Herbert I. Fusfeld and Richard R. Nelson, Editors

Published in cooperation with the Center for Science and Technology Policy,
Graduate School of Business Administration, New York University
Also published as a Special issue of *Technology In Society*, Volume 5, No. 3/4

Pergamon Press
New York   Oxford   Toronto   Sydney   Paris   Frankfurt

Pergamon Press Offices:

U.S.A.   Pergamon Press Inc., Maxwell House, Fairview Park,
                              Elmsford, New York 10523, U.S.A.

U.K.   Pergamon Press Ltd., Headington Hill Hall,
                              Oxford OX3 0BW, England

CANADA   Pergamon Press Canada Ltd., Suite 104, 150 Consumers Road,
                              Willowdale, Ontario M2J 1P9, Canada

AUSTRALIA   Pergamon Press (Aust.) Pty. Ltd., P.O. Box 544,
                              Potts Point, NSW 2011, Australia

FRANCE   Pergamon Press SARL, 24 rue des Ecoles,
                              75240 Paris, Cedex 05, France

FEDERAL REPUBLIC   Pergamon Press GmbH, Hammerweg 6,
OF GERMANY   D-6242 Kronberg-Taunus, Federal Republic of Germany

Copyright © 1984 Pergamon Press Inc.

Library of Congress Cataloging in Publication Data
Main entry under title:

University–industry research interactions.
        (The Technology policy and economic growth series)
        "Published in cooperation with the Center for
Science and Technology Policy, Graduate School of
Business Administration, New York University."
        "Also published as a special issue of Technology In
Society, Volume 5, No. 3/4."
        1. Research, Industrial--Congresses. 2. Industry and
education--Congresses. I. Fusfeld, Herbert I.
II. Haklisch, Carmela S. III. New York University.
Graduate School of Business Administration. Center for
Science and Technology Policy. IV. Series.
T175.U55   1984   338.9   84-2777
ISBN 0-08-030987-9

Printed in the United States of America

Contents

v

Preface

This volume is based on papers and discussions drawn from an international conference on university–industry research interactions held in Stockholm, Sweden, March 7 and 8, 1983. This conference represented the first gathering of leaders in academia, industry, and government from industrialized countries to discuss this subject in a single forum. The objectives of the conference were: to examine mechanisms for cooperation between universities and industry, as well as interfaces between industrial needs and university activities; to compare experiences of different countries and different industry sectors; and to develop recommendations for appropriate actions by both the public and private sectors that could enhance the effectiveness of these mechanisms as a major factor in deriving the optimum benefit from the use of technical resources.

While not exhaustive, the formal papers and discussion summaries contained in this volume reflect a blend of experiences whose goals and structures are useful guides for the intensifying activity in this field. Similarities and contrasts are evident country by country and industry by industry in both the types of mechanisms being pursued as well as the policy questions being asked about the overall purpose and impact of these arrangements on the base of technical competence. Hopefully, the views exchanged at the conference and the insights presented here will serve as a reference for those whose interests and responsibilities require an understanding of industry and national patterns and priority needs expressed by industry and academia for future cooperation.

A major strength of this volume is the distinguished group of colleagues who contributed their thoughts to this effort. We extend our deepest thanks to each author for the time, patience, and responsiveness which the preparation of these papers required. The participation of several senior colleagues in the formal program enlightened and enlivened our discussions and special thanks are therefore due to:

H.B.G. Casimir, Honorary President, EIRMA; former Senior Technical Officer, N.V. Philips Gloeilampenfabrieken, The Netherlands.

Paolo Fasella, Director-General, Directorate-General for Research, Science and Development, Joint Research Center, Commission of the European Communities; Professor of Biochemistry, University of Rome, Italy.

Martin Fehrm, former Director General, National Swedish Board for Technical Development (STU), Sweden.

Gunnar Hambraeus, Chairman, Royal Swedish Academy of Engineering Sciences (IVA), Sweden.

Sogo Okamura, Director General, Japan Society for the Promotion of Science, Japan.

Keishi Oshima, President, Industrial Research Institute, Japan; former Director, Directorate for Science, Technology and Industry, Organization for Economic Cooperation and Development (OECD).

We are also deeply grateful to Trygghetsradet SAF-PTK, Sweden, for providing the major funding for this conference and for their generous cooperation in planning the program and arrangements. In addition, their exceptionally gracious hospitality made the conference a truly memorable occasion. We also wish to express our appreciation to the Royal Swedish Academy of Engineering Sciences (IVA) and the National Swedish Board for Technical Development (STU) for their support. The Organization for Economic Cooperation and Development gave the conference its official patronage.

We would also like to thank representatives of the European Communities (EC), the Industrial Research Institute (IRI), and the European Industrial Research Management Association (EIRMA) for their kind assistance in developing the conference program. We were privileged to have the conference held in the building of the Swedish Association of Graduate Engineers, and we very much appreciated such fine accommodations. The Division of International Programs (INT) of the US National Science Foundation provided a portion of the travel funds for several participants, and we particularly wish to thank Dr. Bodo Bartocha, Division Director of INT, for his continuing interest in the Center's projects.

Herbert I. Fusfeld
Carmela S. Haklisch

University-Industry Research Interactions

A Guide to the Proceedings

Herbert I. Fusfeld
Carmela S. Haklisch

ABSTRACT. Concern for economic growth in the industrialized countries has focused attention on society's use of technical resources. One mechanism for enhancing the effectiveness of the reservoir of science and engineering is university-industry interactions. There are growing indications that such linkages are now becoming more formal, more frequent, more planned. Why is this so? What objectives are served? How can these interactions produce the most effective use of our technical resources to serve universities, industry, and society? These questions are addressed from different viewpoints in the papers contained in this collection. There are different objectives, and, therefore, different emphases from the many countries represented. There are different characteristics for each major industry sector, and there are indications that the nature of the industry is at least as important in determining the degree of university-industry cooperation as the nature of the country. And there are a number of issues of particular interest that call for special attention, such as the role of research institutes or the problems of regional economic development.

The independent, but related, paths of university and industry seem to draw more closely together as the influence of technical change throughout society increases. The steadily growing reservoir of basic science and engineering accumulated from university research has been paralleled by the enormous growth of organized industrial research. Each feeds the other, and linkages have evolved for the transfer of people, knowledge and money.

It seems clear that many pressures have been acting within our technical system to bring about these linkages, and that these pressures have increased since the 1950s. However, one pressure on all the Organization for Economic Cooperation and Development (OECD) countries during the past decade is the concern with economic growth. This, at least, seems to be the simplest reason for the almost spontaneous attention to the subject of university–industry relations that has emerged worldwide during the past three years.

In the United States, a major review of university–industry interactions, "Current US University-Industry Connections," was conducted under the auspices of the Center for Science and Technology Policy, at New York University, as the basis for the National Science Board's 1982 Annual Report, "University/Industry Research Relationships—Myths, Realities, and Potentials." The OECD is completing a review by its own staff to summarize the scope of these activities throughout OECD countries. A joint working group of the US Industrial Research Institute (IRI) and the European Industrial Research Management Association (EIRMA) has addressed this subject. And, in addition, NATO's Scientific Affairs Division has focused particular attention on exchanges between university and industry as a mechanism for developing cooperation and for transfer of ideas and methods. A new program based on this type of exchange was recently initiated in 1982.

Since the attention and interest is evident throughout industrialized countries, some analysis of which factors are common and which are unique to one country would sharpen our understanding of the process. This is the motivation for bringing together informed representatives from many countries to share their experiences and judgments.

The Conference described in these papers does indeed reflect the underlying economic pressure, but with different degrees of directness. The thread that ties together government policy-makers, university scientists, and industrial research executives is the belief that the generation and use of technical change, *i.e.*, innovation, can be a contributing factor in industrial growth, hence in relieving economic problems. Therefore, each country must make the most effective use of its technical resources. One clear mechanism for doing so is cooperation between university and industry.

What Objectives Are Served?

In the past, this cooperation has been largely informal, though of great value to both sides. There are growing indications that such linkages today are becoming more formal, more frequent, and more planned. Why is this so? What objectives are served? How can these interactions produce the most effective use of our technical resources to serve universities, industry, and society?

These questions are addressed from different viewpoints in the papers contained in this collection. There are different objectives, and, therefore, different emphases, in the many countries represented. There are different characteristics for each major industry sector, and there are indications that the nature of the industry is at least as important in determining the degree of university–industry cooperation as the nature of the country. And there are a number of issues of particular interest that call for special attention, such as the role of research institutes or the problems of regional economic development. These different approaches defined the structure of the Conference, and provided a convenient basis for grouping the papers that follow. This overview chapter is intended as a guide for viewing the papers, not as a summary or a substitute. Hopefully, the overview will serve as a framework to describe and accommodate the broad range of views and experiences presented.

Major Themes Discussed

The interactions between university and industry take place almost entirely within a national R & D system. Such cooperation is, therefore, one element within the complex network which accounts for the process of technical change in each country. Despite the differences between countries, it is important to place the functions of university–industry relations in some perspective with respect to the functioning of the overall R & D system. This task is conducted by **Helmar Krupp** with a structural analysis that describes who performs what kind of research for what purpose and at whose expense.

Any examination of university–industry interactions reveals a rich array of approaches. However, underlying the diversity of mechanisms is the potential of the "leapfrog phenomenon." This results from the "iteration" process, or "feedback" loops, which characterize the continuing progress of science and technology. As **H.L. Beckers** points out, this is the process involving universities and industry in which people and ideas, knowledge and application, "leapfrog" each other on the road to progress. Such a description reflects the basis of university–industry interactions, the traditional role and strengths that each partner brings to the relationship for the synergism of "leapfrogging" to occur. Moreover, it imples the importance of each partner in maintaining its fundamental technical vitality so that projects conducted in parallel are fruitful contributions to the science and technology reservoir, a point which **Jürgen Starnick** underscores in his retrospective of the German experience.

An important factor in many programs of university–industry interaction is the desire to advance simultaneously the dual university role in educating new graduates and advancing technical frontiers. Mechanisms which build upon both functions can produce the optimum benefits from cooperation. The strategic importance of this approach is referred to by **Erich Bloch:** "The partnership of academia and industry is a requirement if industry, especially high technology industry, wants to remain in a leading world position."

One illustration of this trend in the US, discussed by **Bloch,** is the establishment of the Semiconductor Research Corporation (SRC). Another is the Council for Chemical Research (CCR), described by **Robert Lovett.** And still another cooperative approach is an enhanced oil-recovery program in France, presented by **Francis Garnier.**

The SRC is a not-for-profit cooperative effort of the semiconductor industry to meet the needs of that industry for basic technical advances and for professional personnel. It interacts with universities through a proposal and contract mechanism, currently at a level of $11 million annually, and increasing. This compares with expenditures by the National Science Foundation of about $7 million annually in this same area. Thus, the SRC is becoming an important linkage between university and industry in strengthening research facilities, research programs, and education related to semiconductor advances.

A similar purpose and impact is provided by CCR, though different mechanisms of funding are involved. This reflects the broader scope of strengthening the base of the chemical industry generally, whereas SRC is more mission-oriented.

The NTH/SINTEF

An interesting variation of this approach is the NTH/SINTEF model in Norway, which **Johannes Moe** describes. The Norwegian Institute of Technology (NTH) is the only technical university in Norway, and the Foundation of Industrial and Technical Research (SINTEF) is a contract research institute located on the campus of NTH and functioning as a not-for-profit foundation, economically and administratively independent of the university. The staffs of NTH and SINTEF often share leadership in different disciplines as well as laboratories and other facilities. SINTEF performs research for a variety of clients in industry and government and serves as a bridge for NTH to address current, practical issues in addition to the customary scope of university research.

Thus, while the research conducted at SINTEF is not directly in support of the education and training program at NTH, the close interaction provides a multitude of channels for technology transfer:

● New scientific information and newly trained scientists can flow from the university to the research institute;
● The institute can serve as a training ground for new graduates;
● The university link to a contract research institute can enhance the relevance of curriculum development and educational programs; and
● The pooling of expertise between the two can improve the individual competence of each and provide critical mass for a given project at marginal cost.

Career-Long Education

Certain industries and countries identify specific problems, related primarily to professional personnel, as separate from research. There is a heightened awareness in particular circumstances of the need for cooperative programs which focus directly on education. This is especialy true for programs structured to assist career professionals beyond the master's or doctor's degree level. The rapid pace of technical change, and the need to maintain an adequate supply of qualified expertise at the frontiers of development, is making continuing education for professionals — throughout their careers — a necessity. **Ingvar Seregard** discusses this trend and the challenge it poses for both industry and universities. The specific needs of the microelectronics, mechanical engineering, and pharmaceutical industries are discussed by **Erich Bloch, Jørgen Fakstorp,** and **Lois Peters/Ernst Vischer**, respectively.

There are several themes throughout these papers that relate to career-long education:

● Technical professionals comprise a resource critical to the viability and competitiveness of a given industry;
● There is often a short supply of qualified technical professionals in a given industry; and
● The obsolescence factor for technical knowhow in some fields is accelerated while the structure of the fields themselves may be changing, so that lifelong education is a requirement for technical vitality.

In some cases, industry is meeting its own needs. However, the extensive nature of professional education in different industry sectors may indicate opportunities for intensified cooperative activity in this area.

Tie to Economic Growth

While university–industry interactions play a role in industrial growth generally, there are very specific questions related directly to economic development. Among these questions, discussed by **Valentin von Massow** and the panel led by **Robert Chabbal**, are:

- Is the academic community an underutilized resource which could assume an expanded role in stimulating the economy?
- Is it possible to ascertain the influences of universities on economic development?
- To what extent does the university aim to promote economic development?
- Are universities properly equipped and appropriately structured to fulfill this task?
- Does one have to take new measures in order to develop the role of universities in economic development?
- What is being done in order to improve the contribution of universities, particularly with regard to the economic development of small- and medium-sized enterprises?

Common Concerns

All of the activity related to university–industry cooperation, however, has raised concern that the traditional role, strength, and independence of a university, so essential to the technical base, may be threatened by the increasing involvement of the academic community in some of the mechanisms currently in operation. As **Hugo Thiemann** points out: "the actual content of university research and its relevan.ː co non-academic pursuits are acquiring increasing significance. A crucial question in the present context is, then, in what sense, how far, and through what mechanism university research capabilities should be matched with problems of particular industrial significance."

The trend in many countries of decreasing government support for university research, increasing industry support, and steady or declining student enrollments has evoked discussion of whether industry will have an inappropriate influence on the nature and/or direction of university research as a result of more collaboration and higher funding leads. Despite this pattern, government seems likely to continue as the dominant source of funding in most cases. For example, Table 1, showing support for university research in the US, indicates that in 1981 industry accounted for less than 4% of the support for university research and development while the federal government provided 65%.

Discussions at the Conference revealed that more fundamental concern has arisen in arrangements where the magnitude of funding is in the order of millions of dollars from a single industrial source, often spread over several years. In these areas, the research may be related but not integrally tied to the education function, and mechanisms have been established for the university to obtain income through patent and licensing schemes or even equity participation in a company. Under these conditions, questions have focused specifically on:

TABLE 1. University R & D Expenditures in the US.*

	1953	1970	1979	1981(est.)
Total University R & D	$255	$2,335	$5,183	$6,300
Funded by Federal Government	$138	$1,648	$3,432	$4,100
Funded by Industry	$ 19	$ 61	$ 194	$ 240
% Federal Government	54%	71%	66%	65%
% Industry	7.5%	2.6%	3.7%	3.8%

*In millions
Source: National Science Foundation, "National Patterns of Science and Technology Resources,"
1981.

- The level of faculty involvement and potential conflict of interest with university responsibilities;
- The involvement of graduate students if the work is not directly related to their educational program;
- The free flow of information; and
- The impact on the overall research program of a university.

Approaches are evolving to address these issues so that mechanisms which preserve the fundamental role of the university can be pursued.

For a summary review, **Duncan Davies** offers a checklist of actions to strengthen university–industry cooperation:

- Accentuating the positive and ignoring the unhelpful majority
- Understanding the drives and constraints; living together; pursuing the counter-cultural
- Selecting, rejecting, and phasing
- Learning from others
- Making things work and sell well
- Raising the patient long-term money
- Creating the right agencies; technology parks; takeover procedure.

His discussion of the process underlying these headlines includes three critical factors which contribute to each of the actions at different points and in varying degrees: the original, innovative, oddball contribution; the generation of consensus to move beyond the first phase; and the sharing and transfer of knowledge.

Looking Ahead

"The sharing and transfer of knowledge" is, in essence, the leapfrog ingredient. Having come full circle from **H.L. Beckers's** discussion, the obvious question is: Where do we go from here?

It is clear that university–industry cooperation will intensify. It seems equally clear that the role of such activity will be different in each country and in each industry. Most important, this cooperation can produce optimum results only when it is tailored to and implemented by each country and each industry, in fact, by each corporation. Nevertheless, there is an important role for collective industry action, and this, too, can be expected to increase where appropriate.

The increasing awareness by each partner of the value and needs of the other is an important requirement for progress and an important safeguard against abuse. The process of technical change is complex, but there is no reason to believe it will be weakened by open exploration of linkages between the university and industry. Certainly industry, however self-sufficient, is becoming more knowledgeable in adapting the advances of universities. Exposure of university faculty to the structure and the problems of industry will broaden the intellectual options available for university research.

The Conference, presented in these proceedings, permitted an exchange of experiences. Each organization, public or private, in each country will exercise its own judgment as to what adaptation of these experiences can be helpful in future activities.

Preamble

H.B.G. Casimir

I am well aware of the fact that many things have changed since I took my doctor's degree more than half a century ago, but all the same I cling to some of my old ideas and ideals. Let me speak about some of them.

Universities should be the centers where really new concepts are born and where really new phenomena are discovered. Some of this new "natural philosophy" may sooner or later turn out to be applicable, some of it may not. However, applicable or not, it is an essential part of our culture: Human civilization did not begin when man began to use tools, but when he began to adorn his tools.

In the past, many fundamentally new concepts were formulated by independent scientists, by scientists not tied to any research establishment, but this is getting extremely rare. Einstein working at the patent office at Bern is the one outstanding example in the twentieth century. Far more important is the role played by "non-university" academic research centers, like CERN, Brookhaven, and so on. It is my firm conviction that such centers will only stay alive if they maintain close contacts with universities. I am afraid that this most important aspect of universities is being threatened: by cuts in budgets and even more by silly attempts to manage it "efficiently."

As to the applicable domains, I consider it desirable that universities deal with the most profound investigations, although not necessarily with the most extensive ones. Industry should have the opportunity to fall back on universities — if it wants to really understand what it is doing. Students should be taught fundamental insight rather than a lot of technical detail. I like to think that, broadly speaking, this situation still prevails, but this may be the wishful thinking of an elderly man.

Let me be more realistic. Much university work is neither at the very front nor of the most difficult kind. It consists in supplementing, clarifying, finding new examples, tying up loose ends. It is not different in character from industrial work, although there is a difference in motives for choosing a subject. And, once a specific problem has been chosen, there is no great difference in motivation of the industrial and of the academic research worker. Good research can only be done when the researcher is interested in the problem *per se,* and temporarily forgets about social, industrial, commercial, or political implications. Similarly, I hope that if I ever have to undergo surgery, the surgeon will not be thinking about the social relevance of surgery while he puts his knife into me.

H.B.G. Casimir is Honorary President of EIRMA and former Senior Technical Officer for N.V. Philips Gloeilampenfabrieken, The Netherlands.

It is especially in this last-mentioned area that fruitful collaboration between industry and universities is possible and desirable. Industry can profit by the capabilities available at universities, and universities will find that contacts with industry considerably widen the range of problems that may be tackled.

I hope these short remarks will serve their purpose as an introduction to our discussions.

The Power of Competency in Industrial Development

Curt Nicolin

We have all learned to esteem knowledge as very important in human life in general, not the least in industrial development; the fantastic rate of industrial development is indeed regarded as a result of increased knowledge. But knowledge is passive. To make use of knowledge we need an active process. We need willpower. We need a goal or a direction in which to move. Would it be correct to describe active knowledge as competence? But competence requires even more information. Any process where knowledge is applied relies on information. We used to regard competence as a quality of man, but it is equally a quality of an organization.

The aim of the industrial process is to supply products and services to a market. In the process we use manpower, capital, and energy. Knowledge may be regarded as the major quality or aspect of manpower and capital assets. Even the simplest tool carries a lot of knowledge, much more so for sophisticated machinery: The higher the quality, the higher the prices. In a market, price is generally governed by supply and demand. The industrial process combines the production factors toward a given end. They are then combined with the aim to minimize the cost of the end product. Should, for any reason, the relative prices change, then another combination becomes optimal. The same holds true should any of the production factors change the quality at a given price. Hence, knowledge affects the impact of production factors in the industrial process.

History tells us that the value of production is proportional to the value of the capital assets in industry. For the past century, capital assets have been roughly double the value of annual production.

The indication is that increased capital should promote increased production. There are, however, certain provisos like the right choice of capital assets and the need to use them, as has been convincingly demonstrated in the present crisis. In Sweden, production per man has improved more than tenfold in the last hundred years, whereas the capital for that time has been roughly double the output. More detailed studies reveal that the same relative increase in capital in various industrial countries gives the same growth rate. This proves true regardless of stage of development. My interpretation is that no country has yet reached a stage of development where a lack of knowledge would hinder a normal return on new in-

Curt Nicolin is Chairman of ASEA AB and is Chairman of Trygghetsradet SAF-PTK.

vestment. Another and much trickier question is why certain countries invest more and have higher growth rates than others.

New knowledge creates new opportunities for profitable investment. As a matter of fact, capital equipment is seldom worn out, but becomes obsolete, generally for technical reasons. This means that new knowledge or, more specifically, new techniques develop faster than wear and tear of equipment occurs.

From these observations, it follows that available competence has been extremely powerful in industrial development. And from this, I would like to turn to technical development.

The Risk Aspect

In our time it has become common practice among governments to support not only research but also technical development. Hardly any government in the industrialized world abstains from subsidies for technical development. This gives me reason to try to analyze what makes technical development click. A saying goes: "Necessity is the mother of invention." In other words, there must be a need or a purpose for inventions or technical development. This need can very well be an improved solution to old problems. But if there is no practical aim, there is no need for technical development. One characteristic of technical development is the risk aspect. Risk is predominant. There is no guarantee of success. For success, first a technical target must be met and then the product or service must stand a market test in a market that is only partially known at the outset. There must be a balance between risk and chance. But surely elimination of risk does not necessarily promote technical development; hence, public purchases of advanced technical products are superior to considerations of guarantees to pay the development cost.

All kinds of industrial activity can be more or less efficient. Competition holds actors on the market scene to efficiency goals. But competence for efficiency varies widely. In my view, there is no field of industrial activity where efficiency varies as much as in technical development. In the process of technical development, one always runs the risk of failure. But even among technically successful contenders, cost can vary on a ratio of 1 to 5 and even 1 to 10. Why?

Big organizations have a tendency to spend a lot more for a given technical project than smaller ones do. Moreover, the necessity to succeed seems to keep concentration to the essentials. Another explanation may be that much technical data is freely available. But there are also differences of policy. If you aim at results close to the impossible, the cost has a tendency to skyrocket. In the end, time lost can often offset more than the extra achievement. It takes high competence to plan and to lead advanced technical development. It seems that Swedish industry has often met with success in this respect. (I can mention projects like fighter airplanes, nuclear reactors, telephone exchanges, and automobiles.) The cost is often a small fraction of what is spent for corresponding purposes, for instance, in the United States.

We deal with a combination of necessity and competence. It is a well-known fact that when you spend large sums of money in a meaningful way, it generally takes a longer time to spend larger sums. It is often said that it costs more to speed up a program. That may sometimes be true, but in my judgment it is more often not. In any technical project there is a critical minimum of resources needed. They are, however, a lot smaller than generally anticipated. In a technical team there must at least be one specialist of technical competence in each discipline. But one gains relatively little by having several specialists. What is important is to have a high quality of competence.

Competence, Not Money

All this is less well-known than one might think. I am worried that even in our most successful organizations I often find the argument that large sums of money are required and will solve the problem. No wonder that politicians are prone to this fallacy. It is high competence, not money, that leads to technical success. It may be true that competence can be bought. But that requires that one can identify competence and that one can provide an environment in which competent people can thrive.

This brings me to the motivation of technical development. Do organizations or individuals engage in technical development just because cost is covered? Certainly not. They engage for profit, for fortune, for pride, for fame — or something of that nature. Technical people love to create, but the process of creation is stimulated by the goal, not by guarantees of cost coverage. On the other hand, most organizations and individuals have difficulty refusing grants which are offered, and that is natural. This then leads to the misinterpretation that subsidies are asked for.

Big technical projects need not only competent and risk-taking entrepreneurs, they also need competent risk-taking customers. Public bodies are often the only alternative for an interested, competent risk-taking customer for prototypes and, sometimes, also for whole projects. The tension between supplier and customer is very productive in technical development.

Tax relief for successful ventures over a number of years would, in my mind, be much more stimulating than subsidies. Tax relief for success means that governments only sacrifice direct revenue in case of success. In such a case, government has many indirect revenues stemming from successful projects.

Education and Basic Research

Other important areas for government engagement are education and basic research. It cannot be said often enough how important the quality standard of technical, economic, and management education is for successful industrial development. High quality education thrives in the environment of research. I believe in this combination, which may be in universities.

In technical development, cooperation between university research and technical development in companies can often be very fruitful. It is useful for both parties to get input from a different body with different terms of reference.

Competence is a quality of people or of organizations. To build competent organizations one must always start with competent people. Whether one starts a new venture or company or wants to build competency into an existing organization, the start is competent people.

I have touched upon the value of high-quality education. Competence, however, is also developed by doing, by practice. How does one select competent people? One good way is if they select themselves, if the incentives for success are great enough to encourage many individuals to strive and to work hard to become competent and sometimes take a chance by starting ventures on their own. This process must be supplemented by screening and selection. How do you select and engage competent people before they have demonstrated results? That is an art, and a difficult one. One thing is certain: Promising people must be provided with chances to perform long before we can be sure of their success. Really good people require, above all, confidence as well as reasonable freedom in order to act and create.

My prescription is that politicians, company boards, and managers must provide competent people with incentives, confidence, and the largest possible freedom of action.

Do they?

The Generation of Knowledge in Advanced Countries

George Bugliarello

What We Know About Knowledge

Knowledge in the Age of the Dinosaur and in the Modern State

One of the most fundamental characteristics of a modern industrial country is the deliberate large-scale quest for knowledge. It is intriguing to think that, fundamentally, the situation has not changed from that which faced our early mammalian ancestors. In their long hiding of a hundred million years, during the triassic period, they could survive the dominance of the dinosaurs only by operating at night and forming models of the world around them—the world which they could not see, but only perceive in part through smell and hearing.

Knowledge was the key to survival then and it is the key to survival today. But the difference is that in a modern industrial country the pursuit of knowledge is deliberate, conscious, and carried out on a large scale. An element of knowledge truly of major concern is knowledge which is useful (or perceived to be such) for technological or economic purposes. Such knowledge is pursued both deliberately and on a large scale: Deliberately means that the process is felt to be too precious to be left to accident or to the inclination of scholars; on a large scale means that it involves a substantial cross-section of society. In technologically advanced countries, the number of workers who generate and manipulate knowledge and information has now become the largest segment of the working population. The cost of education—the process which deals, of course, not only with the development of new knowledge, but also with its diffusion—has also become substantial. In the US, it is second only to the cost of health care, and higher than that of defense.

The fact is that in modern states competing with each other economically and militarily, and in the industries that are their sinews, knowledge is power. For this reason, it becomes crucial for a modern society to constantly upgrade the process by which knowledge is generated and utilized, and to single out those issues on which the successful acquisition and utilization of knowledge will critically depend in the future. The task is far from easy; knowledge is so multifaceted and its use so pervasive that in our societies there is no single focus for dealing with it.

George Bugliarello is President of the Polytechnic Institute of New York.

Knowledge: The Elusive Value

Perhaps the core of the problem is that—more than two thousand years after Plato and in spite of Descartes, Kant, and Chomsky—the concept of what knowledge is continues to remain elusive. This is so because knowledge ultimately depends on the organ that deals with it—the human brain—which is still full of unknowns.

But the lack of a generally agreed upon definition of knowledge that would satisfy biologist, psychologist, linguist, philosopher, physicist, and engineer alike has not prevented us from categorizing knowledge—e.g., basic vs. applied, hard science vs. soft science, embodied knowledge (in a process or product) vs. disembodied knowledge (in a patent or a book), and so on. Neither has this lack of definition stopped us from putting a value on knowledge, or from buying, selling, stealing, and even taxing it, or from learning to store and retrieve it. However, knowledge can be not only gained, but also lost: Witness what happened to the Roman know-how and to classical knowledge during the middle ages, witness the difficulty we have in remembering the simpler technologies of yesterday and applying them to the needs of developing countries.

In recent years we have learned a great deal about how we acquire knowledge and how we can manipulate and transfer it. Some of what we have learned is rather profound and fundamental; the rest is more empirical, but no less useful. We have learned, for instance, that the quest for knowledge is enhanced by the setting of major goals—under the pressure of necessity or ambition—or by the jolts to a nation or a company to invent or perish (as is the case in modern war and in modern technological competition, and as has been the case throughout our biological evolution), or by the push–pull relationship between technology and marketing, or by the rewards and social esteem afforded the creators of new knowledge. (Yet the social supremacy bestowed in certain societies to the quest for basic knowledge over that for its applications has had unfortunate consequences when imitated by developing nations).

By Question and Error

Perhaps the most fundamental fact we have learned about knowledge is that we acquire it by asking questions and by making mistakes.

The questions we need to ask today are not only the *provable* questions—the "Why?" and "How?" (the scientific) questions or the "How to?" (the technological) questions—but also the *prospective* questions such as, "What will we know at a given date in the future?" The quest for answers to the latter—imprecise as they may be—has become a legitimate and sophisticated component of the acquisition of knowledge. Industries and government alike have an ever more urgent need to be prepared for the "future shocks" created by rapid technological change.

Equally important, although at this moment still embryonic, is the quest for *hypothetical* questions. The answers to "What if a certain event will occur?" can accelerate the quest for provable knowledge if we are willing to take the risk of starting up a number of parallel lines of inquiry that will become useful only if other knowledge is acquired.

The importance of questions and errors is pervasive in all our knowledge-acquiring activities, and yet it is much too often overlooked. The latitude in asking questions and making mistakes ought to be a far more relevant criterion in drawing distinctions between university and industry than the conventional emphasis on basic versus applied research. Industry, by necessity, must be more focused than the university. Industry has specific production goals and cannot afford too many mistakes, as they can be very costly once they are embedded in products. Neither can industry easily operate with a climate where authority — intellectual or managerial — is constantly challenged. In the university, on the other hand, it is easier to ask wider and provocative questions and people should not be afraid to make mistakes (they should actually be denied tenure if they play it safe). The genius of an intelligent and productive industry–university interaction lies on a perception, on both sides, of this essential difference.

Given the importance of asking questions, it might also be useful to organize searches for new questions, in the same way that we have organized the communication of new knowledge — that we publish, for instance, annual surveys of new scientific and technological questions and that we reward the authors of the best and most fruitful ones.

Knowledge by Rejection

As a corollary of the fundamental role of asking questions and making mistakes, we have now come to accept the fact that knowledge is gained not by accretion but by a process of constant rejection of older theories (*e.g.*, Popper). The consequences of this are not only theoretical, but also practical — and far reaching. Progress in the acquisition of new knowledge demands a constant questioning of the *status quo* of knowledge. Environments that encourage this are bound to be more successful in generating new knowledge than those that do not. (Unfortunately, at times, the questioning of existing knowledge is perceived by established researchers — who may forget that they were the rebels of yesterday — as a personal challenge to them).

The Modeling Society

As a second corollary, the quest for ever more sophisticated models of phenomena acquires great importance (a quest that, as we have seen, has origins in our deep biological past). The fact is that a modern society is a modeling society. Its survival from nuclear war or from worldwide hunger truly depends on the quality of its models.

The models we are constructing today have progressed from simple cause–effect relationships dealing with an aspect of a single phenomenon to complex sets of interlocking systems and equations, through which we hope to find the answer not only to physical or biological phenomena — such as weather predictions or the onset of cancer — but also to crucial sociotechnological problems such as the impact of automation on employment, or, indeed, the outcome of a military conflict.

An intriguing feature in the development of models is the growing influence of the biological sciences as models for scientific and technological development (*e.g.*, Bugliarello, Businaro), where once only the physical sciences were considered.

The Happy Hunting Grounds for Knowledge

Models are a way of asking questions, but the places where the happiest hunting ground for questions are located are at the interfaces between phenomena, dimensions, processes, or disciplines. We have seen recently, for instance, the combination of genetics and molecular biology give birth to genetic engineering; the combination of optics and electronics give birth to fiber optics; and that of polymers and electronics give birth to organic memory elements. In a more applied domain, we have seen the combination of computers and mechanical machines give birth to automation. Automation, in turn, is giving great impetus to new quests for basic knowledge, because to learn to automate is to focus in very fundamental ways on how we move, how we sense, how we make decisions.

Thus, *where* we focus the search is perhaps the most important strategic decision we can make in the acquisition of knowledge. Today, some of the most promising areas, technologically, are at the submicron level, significant for VLSI circuits; while in physics they are at the subatomic level, and in biology between the atomic and the micron level. Tomorrow, new areas, new dimensions, new phenomena are bound to become important. We can expect, for example, that focus on ways to accelerate the rate of enzyme reactions will greatly enhance the application of genetic engineering to chemical engineering. We can also expect that a deeper understanding of the complementarities between living systems and machines will have a seminal impact on health care, agriculture, and engineering alike, as well as on the education process.

People and Networks

The search for knowledge, of course, is carried out by people, directly or indirectly. Knowledge requires intelligence, and *vice versa*. Thus, modern countries are constantly endeavoring to test and understand intelligence and the learning aptitudes of their citizens. If the results are disappointing, major national debates can ensue.

Endeavors to understand how our minds work have far-reaching implications. For instance, the strong indication that intelligence is critically dependent on the interplay of short- and long-range memory (the latter the cumulation of our learning experience) (*e.g.*, Hunt) suggests the importance of cultivating that interplay in our education process—hence, conceivably, the importance of memorization, today so much in disfavor.

The importance of the interplay between short- and long-range memory also suggests strategies for the design of knowledge networks, in which the long-range memory is constituted by the data banks that are now so rapidly growing in number and diversity. The collective intelligence of a modern society will depend more and more on the nature and quality of the interplay between such data banks and the computing power increasingly available to each of its citizens. Hundreds of millions of people interconnected in Europe, Japan, or on the American continent via personal computers and data banks will constitute knowledge networks of immense power, capable of interacting in real time and with only one order of magnitude less nodal points than the human brain — but with the nodal points now constituted by entire human brains rather than single neurons.

The power of these networks will lead inevitably to ever more frequent attempts at finding ways to automate the proof of scientific theories and the derivation of new knowledge from existing knowledge. The formal derivation of new knowledge is already finding practical embodiment in the INFER program, which is a key feature of the generation of computers now on the drafting boards. In turn, the search for proofs may lead to the quest, still very embryonic, of how to overcome the limitation intrinsic in the nature of mathematics as a set of hypotheses rather than as an absolute logic discipline.

The Training of Researchers

By necessity, modern countries pay much attention to preparing researchers and maintaining them at the cutting edge of their fields by providing them with research support, with further training, and with opportunities for exchanges with their peers. In addition, major efforts are made to keep the *users* of the knowledge developed by the researchers abreast of the latest advances.

The system of training scientists and engineers, usually articulated in several stages, seems by now fairly well codified, albeit with marked differences among countries (*e.g.,* Weber). Most countries seem satisfied with it, but it is fair to say that the system pays only marginal attention to creativity, being more concerned with analysis and the mastery of a commonly agreed upon body of knowledge. It is imperative that the system be challenged. Although not everyone can or should be an innovator, there is a need for a determined effort to train a substantial number of people to develop knowledge, without the constraints of orthodoxy and disciplinary boundaries, by taking utmost advantage of what we know about the psychology of thinking and inventing.

Issues and Concerns

Costs and Expectations

Modern societies, for all their sophistication, are still far from taking full advantage of what they have learned about knowledge and its acquisition. This is not only very costly, because it is inefficient, but also potentially destabilizing, because it may make it impossible to meet the rising expectations of the general population.

The costs of technologically or economically useful knowledge have become very substantial and keep growing. Suffice it to compare the simplicity of the laboratory of Pasteur at the end of the last century with the complexity of that of a molecular biologist today, or the cost of an astronomical laboratory hoisted in orbit by the space shuttle with that of the observatories of Galileo or Tycho Brahe.

A very significant portion of the cost of knowledge is people's cost. For example, on the basis of extremely rough and conservative assumptions, the total cost of educating and training the over 500,000 engineers and scientists in the US involved in R & D—who represent the major group of knowledge workers—comes to some $40 billion. This is the principal investment in the US in human capital for the generation of technological and scientific knowledge. The corresponding figure for the over 3.5 million R & D workers worldwide would come to some $250 billion.

Figures such as these imply that increases or decreases in the productivity of knowledge workers and in that of the training process translate into very substantial gains or losses in the R & D process alone, aside from even higher costs of foregone opportunities and inefficient or faulty application of knowledge. The figures also suggest the importance of the quest for international and intercompany cooperation in the R & D and training process, to avoid unnecessary duplication. (In basic research, however, a certain amount of duplication is necessary to validate theories and to stimulate competition; in applied research and in development, of course, the demands of commercial and military competition tend to limit—but not exclude—the possibilities of collaboration).

A corollary to the high cost of new knowledge is the quest by competitors, adversaries, trading partners, and developing nations for possession of that knowledge at the lowest possible cost. Information has value. Thus another facet of the concern for knowledge in the modern state is the development of policies for technology transfer, to encourage it in certain cases and to discourage it in others. The importance of such policies can hardly be overstated—but the policies are fraught with ideological and practical shoals. Examples are the recent debates over the "Jones Intelligence Doctrine" as a proper mechanism for knowledge acquisition by Third World countries (Dedijer, Branscomb) and the debates over the Soviet gas pipeline, or, in the US, over the disclosure of basic research findings. The fact is that knowledge transfer can be big and sensitive business which tends to involve more and more the national intelligence agencies, such as the CIA or the KGB. Also, it is no longer possible for major elements of knowledge not to be transferred between modern countries, contrary to what happened, for example, between Europe and China between the 16th and the 19th centuries.

The danger of destabilization associated with today's knowledge stems from the dramatic contrast between the high costs of the acquisition of knowledge and the rapidly decreasing costs of its transmission. Low transmission costs give our society an insatiable hunger for knowledge—for new materials to fill the capacity of its numerous transmission channels. This has become painfully evident to the electronic media, with their constant quest for new programs, and may begin to haunt scientific researchers as well. "Future shock" may be just as much a negative shock wave of too slowly fulfilled expectations as a positive shock wave due to new knowledge.

Barriers

The barriers that slow down the useful application of what we have learned about knowledge, and thus contribute to high costs, are primarily human ones—sociological, institutional, organizational. A good example is the still relatively poor communication in a number of countries between industry and the university. In spite of all the focusing on the issue in recent years, the last report of the US National Science Board—while encouraging in terms of the initiatives currently being developed in the US—shows how much remains to be done even in a country where the barriers between university and industry are traditionally not too forbidding (National Science Foundation).

Part of the remedy may lie in resisting an equating of organizational boundaries with people boundaries—that is, in encouraging as fluid as possible a movement of researchers among universities, research laboratories and industry. Another part of the remedy may also lie in involving periodically all the elements of an R & D establishment in the common pursuit of an ambitious knowledge goal—as Prince Henry the Navigator did in Portugal at the beginning of the 15th century to create the foundations of modern navigation, or as NASA did in the second half of this century to reach the moon.

In addition to industry, the university, and the autonomous laboratory, there is a fourth element of the knowledge acquisition system which should not be overlooked: the independent inventor. Independent inventors are perceived today by the scientific establishment to be unable to operate as seminally as their predecessors—an Edison, a Marconi, or an Ericsson—in a high technology environment. They also receive very little encouragement from government policies, except for the sometimes dubious protection of the patent system. Perhaps this is so, at least in part, because independent inventors are not always able to speak the formalized language of the academician or of the engineer in industry (a handicap that the personal computer may remove). Yet Ed Land has shown how, even today, an independent inventor can revolutionize an area of technology.

What Do We Do with Obsolete Knowledge?

There are still many other barriers with which we must come to terms in order to be effective in the acquisition of knowledge. For instance, if we accept the fact that knowledge proceeds mostly through revolutions rather than accretion, new knowledge makes previous knowledge obsolete. It then becomes important to eliminate old knowledge as rapidly as possible. The world is full of drugs proven useless by new developments, full of inefficient designs that perpetuate high rates of energy consumption in buildings, and full of wasteful agricultural practices. These and other examples are, in effect, costly failures of the process of transmission and adaptation of new knowledge.

We need symposia to assess systematically the stubborn survival of the backwaters of old knowledge—particularly in areas of consumer ignorance or where there is no strong industrial or military competition—just as much as we need symposia for new knowledge.

Who Owns the Knowledge, and How Do We Protect Knowledge?

The patent system was developed to encourage the diffusion of the fruits of invention. It now seems to be losing that function in the US because of new attitudes toward patents by the courts. For instance, in a recent decision a US Court of Appeals ruled that the patent in question had no validity since what it tried to protect would have been invented in any case (*Roberts* vs. *Sears*).

As a result, the advice that some patent lawyers now tend to give to their clients is not to build their business strategy on the existence of a patent, but to protect knowledge through confidentiality and trade secrets. The correlate is also a new, more aggressive attitude toward utilizing the knowledge developed by public agencies such as NASA, which until recently was shunned because of public ownership.

Who is Responsible for the Generation of Knowledge?

In a centralized state the answer is simple, at least in principle, and the question becomes one of which branch of the state should do it. In a market economy the answer is more difficult. But even there, a modern state takes a major responsibility for the health of the quest for knowledge, for the development of basic knowledge and for the encouragement of the development of knowledge in industry.

Regardless of type of economy, there almost inevitably arise major tensions connected with the acquisition of knowledge that often are not easily resolved and that can spell the difference between a successful and an indifferent performance in that task. Examples are the tensions between the support of education and that of research, between the support of universities and that of industry or national laboratories, between the satisfaction of urgent social needs and the financing of major research projects, between incentives for innovation versus incentives for production and short-range profitability (excessive support of the latter being a major criticism leveled at American industry today), as well as tensions between kinds of incentives. Does one, for instance, reward a new idea, or does one encourage *the pursuit* of a new idea? Is the Nobel prize better than a series of Nobel fellowships?

Kondratieff: Push or Pull?

Finally, and perhaps more fundamentally, is technological innovation an essential input into economic growth, or vice versa? Present surveys of the political and economic pendulum, supported by some interpretations of economic and technological history, indicate the existence of a strong belief that technology is the prime motor of positive Kondratieff waves of economic growth (*e.g.,* Dickson). In this belief, which is shared as an act of faith by scientists and engineers and an act of hope by a number of governments, many countries are making major investments today in the generation and application of knowledge. Some economists, on the other hand, do not see the relation between technology and economic development to be as simple—*post hoc* to be necessarily *propter hoc*. Yet, in the development of knowledge, as in other realms of human affairs, confidence is the crucial ingredient—confidence in the power of knowledge, wisely applied, to improve our society.

Need for Improvement

The acquisition of knowledge is an activity fundamental to the very definition of a modern society. We can take pride in our technological advances and in our insights into the nature of our world, both of which were only dreams at the beginning of this century. Yet, we must also recognize that there is much room for improvement in the process of the acquisition of knowledge as we currently practice it, and that there are grave risks if we are not willing to rise to the challenge of doing so.

To be more effective in our quest for knowledge, we need intelligent and explicit knowledge policies. We need to pay high level attention worldwide to the state of knowledge, as we pay to the state of the economy or the state of international relations. We need to collaborate across nations as well as across institutions to develop a truly global intelligence, because in the acquisition of knowledge synergism is far more profitable than competition. If we do so, we nourish the great and justified hope that the pursuit of knowledge will eventually become the truly deciding factor in driving economics and international relations, rather than vice versa.

Acknowledgment

I am indebted for some of the concepts presented here to discussions with Dr. U.L. Businaro of FIAT, President R. Rines of the Franklin Pearce Law Center, and Professor M. Tribus of MIT.

References

Branscomb, Lewis, M., "A Letter to Steven Dedijer," *Technology in Society,* Vol. 1, No. 3, Fall 1979.

Bugliarello, G., "Technologia" in *Enciclopedia del Novecento,* Istituto dell' Enciclopedia Italiana, Roma (in press).

Businaro, U.L., "Comparing Natural Evolution and Technological Innovation" (manuscript), FIAT Research Center, Torino, 1982.

Dedijer, Stevan "The I.Q. of the Undeveloped Countries and the Jones Intelligence Doctrine," *Technology in Society,* Vol. 1, No. 3, Fall 1979.

Dickson, D., "Technology and Cycles of Boom and Bust," *Science,* Vol. 219 (February 23, 1983), 933–936.

Hunt, Earl, "On the Nature of Intelligence," *Science* (January 14, 1983), pp. 141–146.

National Science Foundation, "University-Industry Research Relationships—Myths, Realities and Potentials," (Washington, D.C.: US Government Printing Office, 1983).

Popper, Karl R., "Conjectures and Refutation—The Growth of Scientific Books," (New York: Harper Torch Books, 1963).

Roberts vs. Sears, 7th Cir., 82-1886, 82-1958 (1983).

Weber, Ernst, "Engineering Education as a Dynamic System" in H. Boehme, ed., *"Ingenience für die Zukunft,"* (Munich: H. Moos Verlag, 1980).

Electronics

Bjorn Svedberg

The idea that science and technology are essential prerequisites for economic growth and that research fuels the necessary advances is nowadays generally accepted. The history of science and technology shows that important causality emanates both from science via technology and vice versa. For example, it is often the problems and ideas arising in industrial development that initiate research efforts and not the other way around.

The current period of economic difficulty has greatly increased interest in promoting research and development activities with the objective of improving a country's industrial competitiveness. Sweden is unique in that the research and development share of the GNP increased during the 1970s more than in other OECD countries such as Switzerland, West Germany, and the United States.

The recent increase in R & D effort throughout the industrialized world gives us good reason to be optimistic about the future. However, to ensure continued favorable development along these lines, we must make the best use of our national resources to this end. The university, through its research and training programs, is a special asset in this process, particularly due to its traditional orientation to investigation of basic phenomena. It is interesting to note that, although the Ericsson Group carries out more research and development within its Swedish companies than all the technical university faculties combined, only a small percentage is devoted to basic studies, whereas some 70% of the research performed at Swedish universities can be so characterized.

There has been considerable discussion promoting the desirability of a free-flowing exchange of the knowledge and ideas generated within the often separate confines of basic research and industrial development. Such an exchange implies direct cooperation between universities and industry with the proposed objective of improving the overall effectiveness of national R & D efforts.

The concept of university/industry cooperation has been discussed so far in general terms, as an idea of abstract interest to industrial sectors. But what are the special characteristics of the electronics sector — research, development, production, or marketing — that require attention if university/industry relationships are to be useful to this specific sector?

Bjorn Svedberg is President and Chief Executive Officer of L.M. Ericsson Telephone Company, parent company of the Ericsson Group.

The following should without doubt be taken into consideration:

- There has been a vigorous decrease in the price/performance factor exhibited for complex electronic components (LSI, VLSI, etc.). The decrease in this factor has been 10:1 every 4 years for the last 15 years, and this development is expected to continue for at least another decade. This, of course, creates a dynamic situation with abundant possibilities for products based on new technical solutions, new products, and new production methods.
- A wider range of electronics industries can be viewed by taking into consideration "small-scale operations" included in the service sector and software houses. In these cases, if good ideas are available, new commercial activities can be initiated with modest capital investments.
- The electronics sector is unprecedented in the way it penetrates all other technical sectors. The number of systems and products with some electronic content is increasing steadily. In many cases, it is just the electronic component that creates the competitive advantage of the product. The possibility of introducing electronics in new areas should, therefore, be held particularly in mind when industry and universities collaborate.

Universities/Industry Cooperation

Universities' research programs affect industrial R & D activity in three different ways:

- indirectly via the university's educational programs,
- directly through cooperative links between companies and universities; and
- as a driving force in the formation of new enterprises.

Let us examine each of these different mechanisms.

Influence Through the Universities' Educational Programs

The main task of the Swedish universities is to educate engineers for Swedish industry. To manage this task satisfactorily, particularly in electronics, the university must be well oriented to international developments in this highly competitive field. This is best achieved by connecting the teaching activity to research.

In American universities, the connection between teaching and research is much stronger than in Swedish universities. MIT, for example, has an Undergraduate Research Opportunities Program (UROP) which gives students a chance to participate in research under competent guidance. Participation in a project may begin at any time during the academic year and may last from one term to two years.

Within Swedish universities, the connection between training and research has been weakened primarily for the following reasons:

- A formal organization has emerged in which questions of research and training are handled separately.
- There has been a continual lack of resources for training purposes, in favor of funding research and the acquisition of information. Aggravating the problem

of an already inadequate capacity for training throughout the university system is the current requirement by the expanding electronics sector for large numbers of well-trained graduates.

• In addition, both research and training have lagged behind industry due to the extremely dynamic development in the electronics domain.

These factors have contributed to an environment within the university that does not inspire students to choose careers in academic research. To this may be added the fact that in the competition between universities and industry in recruiting people with the requisite knowledge and abilities, industry can offer more attractive conditions of employment.

All these conditions taken together undermine the effectiveness and competence of university research. Indeed a vicious circle is created because industry disparages the university as a research partner, thereby deteriorating the prospects for university development.

This process must be changed. This can only be done through government action directed toward lessening the gap between the favorable conditions of employment found in industry and those described in the university environment summarized above.

This is, of course, a difficult period of economic constraint. In the case of priorities, the quality of research should go before quantity. Quality in research cannot be ordered through ambitious sectoral programs or through any other form of rigorous control; it is very much dependent on individuals. Despite the fact that elitist thinking is not *comme il faut* in today's society, the status of university research must be raised so that more of the superior scientists and engineers choose academic research for a career. How this is to be achieved and in what way industry can contribute should be an urgent subject for debate. This debate should also include the importance of international cooperation.

Direct R & D Links Between Industry and Universities

• *Increased Flexibility in Universities.* Compared with many industrial countries —and especially the US—the research results of technical universities are utilized to a relatively small degree in Sweden. Commissioned research is only 4–5% of the total support in our two major universities, KTH and CTH. This is partly because collaboration between industry and research scientists has taken other forms, *i.e.,* the research institutes.

The basic reason that only limited university/industry cooperation exists today is undoubtedly the traditional perception that this type of interaction was a dubious business. Today, such working relationships are viewed quite differently. They are considered not only fully legitimate but, in fact, highly desirable. This should mean that the time has now come for a review of university work methods and organizational structure. Bureaucracy and formalism must be reduced so that the universities can respond with enough flexibility to keep pace with the dynamic development of the electronics fields.

For example, our system for appointing professorships is obsolete in today's environment. Perhaps, professorships should be held only for a limited period, in order to be sure that such positions are filled by those at the forefront of their field. Other faculty appointments outside of the areas of dynamic technical change should also be made only for limited periods.

Universities should have greater autonomy within the framework established by the Office of the Chancellor of the Swedish Universities. A university should have the flexibility and authority to decide on appointments of professors and the distribution of resources among different faculties.

● *Increased Flexibility in Cooperative Mechanisms between Industry and Universities.* Efficient research at universities is advanced through a dialogue between the universities' research, and the development activities of industry.

One way of encouraging this dialogue would be to create increased opportunities for temporary transfer of staff in either direction between universities and industry. Unfortunately, different salary levels might make such exchanges difficult. In order to reduce this barrier, salary schedules of professors and research managers must be raised to better match the industrial pay scale, even though salaries for technical faculty are no longer consistent with nontechnical faculty. Furthermore, in many of the applied sciences, it would be a distinct advantage for professors, research managers and lecturers to have industrial experience. Finally, increased interaction requires a positive attitude towards its benefits on the part of both the parties directly involved, and their respective administrations.

Advantages of Increased Links Between Industry and Universities from Industry's Viewpoint

There are several advantages of more cooperative mechanisms between industry and universities.

● The development-oriented R & D of industry can be broadened through the universities' basic research-oriented contribution.
● The university can form the basis for interdisciplinary studies, since the university is often involved in a wider range of fields than any individual company.
● The university can perform basic research that is of common interest to several different companies.
● The university can contribute to an important international exchange of knowledge through its international network of contacts. This would provide an excellent complement to what industry itself can acquire through marketing, subsidiary companies, and so on.
● As mentioned in the introduction, electronics components will be introduced to many areas beyond the field of electronics. Many small companies, not in the electronics business *per se,* require a sufficiently strong competence to be able to introduce necessary electronics in their products, often within a limited time. This is an area where the university could assist with professional competence.

Formation of New Enterprises Based on the R & D Activities at the Universities

We all agree that the establishment of new enterprises is very important for a number of reasons. One reason that might become more and more important is the fact that small and new companies generate many more new jobs than do the large ones today. They also seem to be more efficient in their use of R & D money and it is, therefore, my belief that we must create a climate that increases the possibilities for new entrants in the labor market to have a full array of opportunities.

The high speed of transfer of scientific results into industrial products in the US is possible because of the open atmosphere that exists between universities and industry, and because a number of mechanisms have been developed which allow interactions to become strong and effective while still leaving each partner free to pursue its respective interests and societal functions. We are on our way in Europe, but I have a feeling that we still have a long way to go to reach the American level of cooperation. A discussion of different national experiences might highlight useful lessons for each of us.

Overview of Policy Issues:
Panel Report on Electronics

Michiyuki Uenohara and Nils Starfelt

The modern electronics industry is rapidly advancing, and its structure is also rapidly changing. It is based on modern science and technology ranging from mathematics and material sciences to systems and software technologies. The science base is very broad: It includes not only the natural sciences but the social sciences as well, and the rate of change in each is high. Spectacular single breakthroughs are still important, but most innovations occur through a large number of improvements in several scientific fields and interdisciplinary interactions. No single company, no country, can cover all the fields of science and technology which form the base of the electronics industry.

R & D within this industry is essential for its growth and vitality. Most of the R & D worldwide is performed by industry, with concentration in applied research and development. Basic research in both the natural and social sciences is conducted at universities which must also educate qualified scientists and engineers for this dynamically changing field. There is, therefore, great potential for interaction between the university and industry.

University Roles

Education and Research

From industry's point of view, the main role of the university is education. High-quality research at universities is viewed as reinforcing high-quality education through training students and providing opportunities for faculty to maintain contact with broader developments. The interaction between universities and industry in this field is particularly important since progress occurs internationally and has often been inspired by the solution of problems originating in outside research laboratories, especially with regard to industry.

Arrangements for cooperation are frequently in the form of research grants or contracts. Other mechanisms might include the sharing of expensive materials,

Michiyuki Uenohara is Executive Vice President and a member of the Board of Directors of NEC Corporation, Japan.

Nils Starfelt is Counsellor for Science and Technology at the Swedish Embassy in the United States.

equipment, and/or facilities. For example, research required for a doctoral thesis could be performed in an industrial laboratory, a widespread practice in Holland and Sweden.

Source of Information

In addition to research and education, the university can perform a function critical to the electronics industry — that of an international clearinghouse of new information. University scientists generally have an extensive network of international contacts. Coupled with interdisciplinary contacts, this comprises a valuable reservoir of knowledge; the university could perform a vital role in the assimilation and dissemination of information of use to the electronics industry, industries utilizing electronics, and some companies just starting up. The Japan Society for the Promotion of Science, for example, has played an important part in cross-fertilizing knowledge between academia and industry by organizing information exchange groups.

Research Consortia

Collaboration between companies is often difficult. In the US, antitrust regulations pose a constraint. In Scandinavia, fierce competition in the small size of the markets among a limited number of companies tends to preclude cooperative efforts. However, in both situations, collaboration in basic, pre-competitive research could be facilitated by the involvement of universities. Such arrangements could optimize the use of funds and technical resources and result in the creation of research teams of critical size to conduct the necessary research more efficiently and effectively. In the US, several research consortia have been established in the field of electronics and most of the research funded by these will be performed at a university. A specific goal of the collaboration is a high standard of excellence in training scientists and engineers.

Exchange of People

One way of using industry experience in the planning of university research is through participation in university boards and research councils. This is done in Sweden.

Another way is to move scientists and engineers in both ways, from university to industry and vice versa. There are several barriers to this type of interaction, such as the fairly large salary differences in several countries. In Sweden, such a system with adjunct professors has proved to be successful. An industry researcher under this plan spends a 20% time commitment as a university professor.

Continuing Education

One of the largest problems envisaged by the electronics industry is the obsolescence of training in its technical personnel. The very rapid change in the technology and knowledge base of this field requires continuous re-education of engineers and scientists. This is a problem that demands much more attention. There do not seem to be any standard plans for continuing education now in operation. Much is done inside companies but there is a great need for more industry–university interaction in an educational program that would continue throughout a career lifetime.

Common Problems

There are several problems that seem common to the experience of many countries.

- Because of the competitive pressures and dynamic nature of the electronics field, and constraints at universities such as obsolete equipment, there is a risk that industry may assume more of the pioneering research. This would leave universities primarily with the role of training graduates, who have little experience with conducting advanced research. Moreover, it would alter the use of technical resources in industry. The negative aspects of such a possible trend are obvious.

- The vicious circle of salary differences is also a problem in many countries. Because of the need for engineers in industry, the salaries in industry are higher than in universities. It is thus difficult to recruit good graduate students for university research, which in turn leads to a shortage of qualified Ph.D.s to fill vacant professorships and to train the next generation of needed engineers. However, the shortage of scientists and engineers in electronics may be exaggerated. The system is somewhat elastic in the sense that companies can use engineers with basic education other than the customary specializations. Different countries have different concerns related to the training of Ph.D.s. In Sweden there is no visible labor market in industry for Ph.D.s. As a consequence the interest among new graduates to continue to a Ph.D. degree is not very high.

The importance of the electronics industry to the economy of each country is strategic. This industry demands a broad and constantly revitalized science and technology base which even the largest companies cannot sustain alone. University–industry interaction is, therefore, a necessary mechanism for strengthening each nation's technical base in this field. The complementarity of the university role in educating professionals and conducting frontier research and of industry's role in development of new products and processes is one which should be enhanced. While distinctions in these roles are often not sharply defined, the basic functions of the two communities provides a balanced system of technical resources. Cooperative endeavors which serve to facilitate communication and improve the technical competence of each can, in turn, serve to improve the effectiveness of the overall system.

Pharmaceuticals

Lois S. Peters

The technical base and complexity of the pharmaceutical innovation process provide many points of contact for, and often necessitate, interactions between universities and companies. These factors can hinder interactions, as well. The importance of the regulatory process to the pharmaceutical industry and to interactions between government and pharmaceutical firms, and government and university complicates university interactions with this industrial sector. On the one hand, the regulatory process is a factor in drawing the parties together, and, on the other, it can restrain or limit the scope of university/pharmaceutical company research interactions.

Pharmaceutical firms have a tradition of extensive contacts with academic researchers. An explanation lies in several special characteristics of the pharmaceutical industry, such as:

- The high level of basic research within major pharmaceutical firms;
- The high concentration of scientific and engineering personnel relative to the total number of employees; and
- The dependence of drug companies on medical schools in order to follow government-mandated testing regimes for their new drugs.

Research and new product development are particularly important for competition among the major pharmaceutical firms (National Academy Press, 1983). Basic research, which—at least in most subject areas—is conducted primarily at universities, is funded at a high level "in-house" within this industry. One recent estimate suggests that about 12% of the pharmaceutical research performed in the United States is basic (Charles River Associates, 1981). Another study showed that, in 1975, the US pharmaceuticals spent 5.1%, 38.6% and 56.3% of their total R & D expenditures on basic research, applied research, and development, respectively (Nason and Steger, 1978).

In the United States, the ratio of research and development scientists and engineers per thousand employees is quite high in the drug industry, with an average over the past five years of 62 per thousand. This ratio in chemicals and allied products is 41 per thousand, while the average ratio over all industries is 27 per thousand (*Chemical and Engineering News,* 1981).

This focus of the pharmaceutical firms on basic research, and their continuing need for highly qualified professionals makes them natural allies of universities.

Lois S. Peters is Senior Program Director at the Center for Science and Technology Policy, New York University.

These two sectors in fact do have extensive networks of interaction throughout the world. In the past, the form which this interaction has taken is informal networking, rather than formal research agreements. Pharmaceutical ties with universities are primarily through personnel exchange, personal contacts, and participation in scientific conferences and advisory committees. The level of participation in these activities is probably greater for the drug industry than most other industries. Many drug companies have 100 or more university consultants on retainer. In the United States, in comparison to other industrial sectors, many pharmaceutical firms supply on company salary, free to the university, a relatively large number of adjunct professors (30–75) to university departments (Peters and Fusfeld, 1983a). Pharmaceutical companies sponsor many scientific and technical meetings, and they also send their scientists regularly to such meetings, seminars and workshops.

In a recent study is was observed that a high degree of US university/industry cooperation in pharmaceuticals is characterized by a high degree of university/industry sectoral mobility (Peters and Fusfeld, 1983a). In the US, in recognition of the significant federal monies that have gone into basic research and into the establishment and maintenance of programs to train scientists, this mobility also includes linkages to the National Institute of Health.

Safe and Effective Products

Pharmaceutical research is characterized by substantial risks and lengthy time requirements. The desired outcome, of course, is a safe and effective therapeutic product or preventive medicine. Potentially useful drugs must be tested in animals for pathological and toxic effects. Once the efficacy and safety of new drug candidates has been proved in animals, these substances must undergo a series of clinical trials to demonstrate and examine basic pharmacological effect and safety in humans. Both these areas of applied research benefit from the alliance of a pharmaceutical firm and a university. In fact, conditions frequently necessitate this alliance. In the United States, the money spent at universities for clinical trials and meeting government regulations is usually in the form of applied contract research. However, in some instances, these large contracts also provide researchers with extra funds which enable them to conduct basic research programs (Peters and Fusfeld, 1983a).

While pharmaceutical firms spend large sums of money on basic research in-house, in the US, the amount spent on basic research at universities is a small percentage (2%) of pharmaceutical firms' total R & D expenditures. The money spent on clinical trials at universities, funded by pharmaceutical firms, is about ten times the amount of funds provided by these firms for basic research at universities (Peters and Fusfeld, 1983a).

Recently worldwide, there has been considerable extended effort in research in the pharmaceutical industry. This may reflect the continuing increase in cost for innovation. The increasing complexity of pharmaceutical innovation, recent developments in academic research, and the increasing cost of taking new products through the government regulatory process, suggest that one way of combating such difficulties is to increase cooperative research efforts, particularly with academic researchers.

New developments have pointed to the importance of a wide variety of disparate subjects — biochemistry, fermentation technology, electronics, computer science, physiology of disease — to basic research and to development of health care products. Most firms cannot afford to have the depth of expertise needed in all these subject areas, thus they must look outside the firm for help. New types of research teams must be formed.

Currently, there are many subject areas for fruitful university–industry research cooperation. For example the biological action of many molecules is not well understood. While we can test a substance to determine if it will taste sour (*e.g.*, PH), we do not have a suitable test to determine if a substance will taste sweet. Immunology and cell biology are two additional important areas that merit extensive research cooperation. Another area is three-dimensional computerized modeling of molecules and molecule systems. Computerized biological data bases could generate a new wave of pharmaceutical research. Much of the expertise in creating such a data bank and knowledge of the quality of the input resides within the university.

Expanding Cooperative Research

With respect to the expansion of cooperative research activities between universities and pharmaceutical firms there are several domains of consideration.

- The implications of new developments in molecular biology and their impact on drug development;
- Research training and production of new doctorates;
- The importance of patents and proprietary rights;
- The changing relationship of public authorities to pharmaceutical institutions; and
- The impact of increased university/industry research cooperation on issues involving drugs.

Recently many small companies have sprung up to exploit advanced techniques in cell fusion and manipulation of the genetic material of the cell for development of new health care products. In the United States alone, there are approximately 200 such firms, many of which were founded by academic researchers, or which involve the active participation of university scientists through their membership on company advisory boards (Peters and Fusfeld, 1983b). This involvement of university researchers in commercialization of their own basic research may affect the nature and direction of research at those universities where scientists are playing a particularly active role.

Several large firms have either bought genetic engineering firms or negotiated research agreements with these new small firms (Peters and Fusfeld, 1983b). Such interaction may impact traditional relationships between pharmaceutical firms and universities.

New Doctorates

Research and training and the production of new doctorates has always been a central thread of common research concern between universities and companies. The rapid pace of new developments point out the need to greatly increase the flow and exchange of personnel between various sectors. If you look at the correlation between the age of M.D.s and the drugs they prescribe, the M.D.s tend to select drugs that were invented when they were 35. This suggests that there are opportunities for continuing education for practicing professionals. The interdisciplinary character of the emerging biotechnology industry will require individuals with new types of skills (Peters and Fusfeld, 1983b). The nature of biotechnology warrants particular emphasis on interdisciplinary training. In the United States and Britain, college biotechnology programs are on the rise and many companies have participated in their development. A concern among some industrialists and academics is that these courses are "trendy" and that they may not provide appropriate training for and entry into lasting and satisfactory careers in biotechnology. The uncertainty of the numbers and types of technicians that will be needed in the future make analysis of such developments difficult, yet, for the most part, industry sources say the skills taught in the programs give students an advantage (Amatniek, 1983).

Patents are considered by pharmaceutical firms to be essential, if a new drug is to be profitable for the company that creates it. Thus pharmaceutical research, by its very nature, requires the development of proprietary information. Hence, there is a continuing compromise in this industry between the tendency of drug companies to cooperate in basic research and to draw back because of proprietary concerns. Legal protection of proprietary rights is extremely important and may explain the smaller amount of cooperative research sponsored by this industry at universities than one would expect from such a highly science-based sector. Because of the importance of patents and proprietary data to new pharmaceutical products, pharmaceutical firms — in funding contracts and grant research at universities — are frequently adamant about obtaining exclusive licenses, if not patents. Expanded university/industry research efforts may compromise access to publicly funded research at universities.

The Relationship of Public Authorities

Several factors in government/industry relationships are serving to promote research cooperation among universities and industry. Since World War II in most Western nations, the relationship of public authorities to pharmaceutical institutions has changed in three major ways. They have become *customers* in the sense that major responsibility for health care costs is assumed by governments; they have become *guardians,* because, as knowledge of human biochemistry has increased, a greater public awareness of the danger of drugs has emerged, and governments have developed regulatory apparatus in response. Finally governments have become *promoting agents,* because they want to stimulate job creation. There is much increased emphasis on the small firm, its role in job creation, and in technology-based regional development. Currently, governments faced with outrageously increasing health-care costs are seeking ways to combine the interests of companies, the universities and the patients (public), so as to improve cost-benefit ratios to all. Targeting research areas for university—industry cooperation may be a partial answer.

Studies of the costs of various diseases may indicate R & D priorities. For example, if hospitalization is the largest cost component of a disease, and drugs the smallest, an important criterion for support of drug research, in addition to scientific feasibility, should be targeting potential drugs that would reduce hospitalization.

Pharmaceuticals is an industry marked by complicated regulatory procedures, which significantly affect its cost of R & D (Grabowski and Vernon, 1982; Wardell *et al.,* 1978).

In most countries, university scientists act as independent public consultants on issues involving the regulation, safety and efficacy of drugs. But as university/industry relations become stronger, this creates a situation which could reduce the independence and the credibility of the professors. On the other hand, these connections also clearly create a crossing point for public and private interests to meet on neutral ground. To the extent that university experts are merely advisers, the increased university/industry connections present little ground for conflicts of interest. However in most European nations, decisions on approval of new drugs are not solely the responsibility of career bureau officials, but, instead, these decisions are either substantially advised or formally made by committees of independent medical experts.

Some European committees of experts are mandated to review all drug applications and either approve a drug which is shown to be safe and efficacious or recommend to the regulatory agency that a drug should or should not be approved. In three countries—the Netherlands and Norway, and Sweden, these committees have been given the responsibility of making the decision to approve, reject, or withdraw a drug. In the United States, committees are used primarily to provide advice on problems or questions that the FDA may have concerning selected drug applications. There is a current desire in the United States to change the role of these expert committees (National Academy Press, 1983). Thus, all nations should develop guidelines that would not hamper current opportunities for cooperative research, but would ensure the continued independence and objectivity of professors, and, thus, the credibility of the university in resolving issues.

Conclusion

In conclusion, there is a history of fruitful cooperation between university scientists and pharmaceutical firms, and there appears to be ample new opportunities for increased levels of interaction and increased types of interactions. However, as with any change in the *status quo,* there are impacts and issues which must be considered in the interest of maintaining a healthy innovation system.

References

Amatniek, Joan C., "College Biotechnology Programs on the Rise," *Biotechnology* 6(1):497 (1983).

Charles River Associates, "The Effects of Patent Term Restoration on the Pharmaceutical Industry," OTA Report, Boston, Massachusetts, May 4, 1981, p. 56.

"Facts and Figures for Chemical R & D," *Chemical and Engineering News,* July 27, 1981, pp. 47-71.

Grabowski, Henry, and John Vernon, "The Pharmaceutical Industry" in R.R. Nelson, ed., *Government and Technical Progress, A Cross Industry Analysis* (New York: Pergamon Press, Inc., 1982)

Hanson, Ronald, "Estimates of Development Costs and Times and the Effects of Prepared Regulatory Changes" in Robert Chein, ed., *Issues on Pharmaceutical Economics* (Lexington, MA: D.C. Heath, 1979).

National Academy Press, *The Competitive Status of the U.S. Pharmaceutical Industry* (Washington, DC: National Academy Press, 1983).

Peters, L.S., and H.I. Fusfeld (a), *Current U.S. University-Industry Research Connections* (Washington, DC: National Science Board, 1983).

Peters, L.S., and H.I. Fusfeld (b), *Biotechnology in the New York and New Jersey Region: Resources and Future Growth* (New York: New York University Center for Science and Technology Policy, 1983).

Wardell, W.M., *et al.*, "The Rate of Development of New Drugs in the United States," *Clinical Pharmacology and Therapeutics*, May 1978.

Overview of Policy Issues:
Panel Report on Pharmaceuticals

Ernst Vischer

The context for university–industry cooperation in the pharmaceutical field has in some instances been negatively affected by public antagonism toward companies in this industry. While the majority of products produced by these firms benefit the general health of the population, the public's fear of harmful products has tainted the more specialized environment for productive collaboration between the academic and industrial communities. Over the last several years, however, attitudes have become more constructive, and examples of cooperation now exist, particularly in the much publicized area of genetic engineering.

The research focus of cooperation between university and the pharmaceutical industry varies greatly from one particular field to another. Whereas in the strictly medical field the evaluation of new active entities in human beings is in the foreground, frontier scientific experimental work is more dominant in the pharmacological and biological areas.

The type of collaboration is also changing with time. In earlier years, it was often possible that a given chemical substance, particularly natural products, isolated or synthesized in a university laboratory, could be developed easily and directly into a pharmaceutical preparation by the industry. That is unlikely to happen today owing to the complexity of research, proprietary controls, and testing regimens. Thus, whereas collaboration formerly may have taken the form of a joint research undertaking, now the form would involve more of a consulting relationship between a university researcher and pharmaceutical firm.

Proprietary concerns and patent problems are important issues in university-industry relationships. For these and other reasons, industry may want to keep work directed toward the isolation or preparation of active principles and substances in-house and to concentrate cooperation on other areas of research particularly suitable for university research. Such areas may include studies on the mode of action of certain active principles, on receptors and blockers, on metabolic studies, and the like.

There has been considerable attention focused on the establishment of new commercial laboratories based on university research — either as a company started by a university researcher off-campus and separate from a university, or on-campus and bearing some special institutional identity to avoid conflict of interest problems. The longevity of these laboratories and their relationships to universities or to uni-

Ernst Vischer is Vice Chairman of the Board of Directors of Ciba-Geigy.

versity–industry arrangements tied to their establishment may be questionable as a given discovery matures in the innovation cycle. For example, the large costs of pharmacological and toxicological testing and of extensive clinical trials associated with the noninventive research phases may pose too overwhelming a burden for some of the new entrants in the industry.

University–industry relationships in the pharmaceutical industry also involve a key interest — an adequate supply of qualified scientists on which industry research laboratories are highly dependent. Concern has fluctuated between the merits of broad scientific education versus the expertise of a narrow specialty. Better communication between firms and academic institutions on the areas of competence and the scope of flexibility that are needed in the foreseeable future might serve to enhance both the employment opportunities for graduates and research strengths for industry in this highly competitive field.

A possible new area for collaboration rests in education in the use of new drugs for medical practitioners. The progress in the pharmacological, biological, and medical sciences is extremely rapid. The average medical practitioner who left a university some 10- or 20-odd years ago cannot be expected to keep abreast of these advances. Yet, at the same time, the pharmaceutical industry continues to make available products which, in fact, demand a sound familiarity with such new developments. It is, therefore, essential that the dispensers of modern pharmaceutical products be constantly re-educated and kept informed about advances in medical science. This might be a field for collaboration between universities and medical schools, on the one hand, and the pharmaceutical industry, on the other.

Petroleum

Francis Garnier

The French enhanced oil recovery program provides an instructive example of criteria that play an important role in university–industry research cooperation. Such cooperation, however, should be examined in the context of the organization of research in France.

Scientific Research in France

About 290,000 people are involved in R&D, which is 1.2% of the total manpower pool. Among them, 107,000 are research engineers, 41,000 are associated with universities, and 37,000 are associated with private centers. This R&D is carried out by different industry sectors (*e.g.,* chemical, petroleum, electronics), by public research agencies (*e.g.,* CNRS, CEA, INSERM, CNES), and by the universities. Currently the national budget for this effort amounts to 63 billion francs, with 26 billion devoted to the private sector and 37 billion for public research.

Public research employs about 70,000 people. Two primary characteristics are the permanence and continuity of its research positions and long-term financial support of the research projects. This large independence from fluctuations in the economy is a factor which, on one hand, favors the development of high quality fundamental research, but, on the other hand, makes research teams less inclined to move quickly in new research areas. Here appears one of the problems which concerns the financing of a university laboratory in the scope of collaboration with industry. What should be the ideal percentage of financial support from industry, over its total budget, which would attract a research team for working on a defined problem while still preserving the necessary scientific independence? This is a difficult question which depends on the financing structures in each country and also on a given scientific discipline (physics, chemistry, etc.). In France, for instance, in the chemistry laboratories belonging to a university (or CNRS), it is assumed that the mean financial support from private sources should not exceed 30% in order to maintain basic scientific freedom.

With these remarks in mind, we will now analyze the build-up of collaboration between industry and university on a subject corresponding to an important industrial need, enhanced oil recovery.

Francis Garnier is Director of the Solar Photochemistry Laboratory at CNRS in France.

Enhanced Oil Recovery Program

The Problem

Classical oil recovery techniques (natural pressure pumping, water injection, etc.) leave about 50–60% of the oil in the fields; an increase of only 10% in recovery would correspond to the total amount of the oil production till now. When the first oil crisis struck the western countries in the early 1970s, many oil companies thus became very interested in enhanced oil recovery prospects.

In France, ELF Aquitaine started a project in this area. Among various solutions considered, the use of microemulsions appeared promising, but research teams soon encountered basic problems due to incomplete fundamental knowledge in the field.

As these teams turned to the university, a problem arose: Interest in colloidal chemistry had been declining for many years in France, and universities could not afford the specialized competence needed to answer some of the fundamental questions. The problem was to motivate good university research teams to pursue this new scientific area and thus to develop the needed competence in coordination with the needs of industry.

The "Cooperative Research" Program

In 1974, the DGRST, a governmental department in charge of French science and technology policy, set up a "cooperative research" program, called "Microemulsions, Polymer Solutions, and Chemical Processes." This program was led by a committee involving members from both industry and the university. The annual budget was 1.5 million francs per year. Each year the committee proposed a research program which was sent to all universities. Research teams were invited to submit project proposals within this program. Each project had to be sponsored by an industrial partner in order to ensure, on the one hand, the relevance of the problems analyzed, and, on the other, a collaboration between the two kinds of approaches, fundamental and applied.

About ten contracts were thus let each year, the total sum of 1.5 million francs devoted only to equipment, travel, and overhead expenses. All the results were presented and discussed during annual meetings, which were open to everyone.

From 1974 to 1982, this cooperative research program was enlarged to other related research areas, such as the transport and treatment of heavy oils, and the annual budget rose to 4.5 million francs. This program is designed to be flexible and evolutionary in order to adapt to new or changing problems.

Results

The following results are evident after eight years of operation:

- Thirty-five laboratories, belonging to physics and chemistry departments, have been involved in this program, and the total manpower devoted to this research is about 800 individuals.

- While largely undeveloped in France in 1974, the science of colloids and microemulsions has rapidly achieved an international level of distinction with highly competent experts.
- The science and technology of enhanced oil recovery has improved greatly, and some large scale promising experiments have been completed.

Some Comments About the University–Industry Relationship

There are several points one may emphasize which are determinants in the development of such collaboration.

Human Considerations

One of the key problems concerns the gap between the short-term applied needs often expressed in industry, and the long-term fundamental problems taken into account in the university. Close relations must be established between those two worlds in order to reach a mutual understanding between these two kinds of approaches and to benefit from complementarity between them.

Another point relates to the identification of problems and possible solutions. There are often unanswered scientific questions in industry, and at least part of the solution is in the university. But frequently information is not exchanged due to the lack of an appropriate communication link.

Structural Considerations

In order to develop high-quality fundamental research, the necessary freedom must be maintained in research laboratories. Too tight a collaboration on a very limited subject is the other extreme which cannot be advised. Thus, the collaboration structure should be smooth enough to allow a laboratory a high degree of freedom, but selective enough to drive the research toward significant goals.

Overview of Policy Issues:
Panel Report on Petroleum

Moshe Lubin
Gillis Een

To observe that the petroleum industry is a critical element in the economic fabric of the world would be to note the obvious. To suggest that there is a need for a strategy for establishing and maintaining the health of this industry would elicit no significant debate. To conclude that it is desirable to have such a strategy, including university, industry, and government participation, and that this strategy is still evolving would be correct.

The difficulty in arriving at a strategy linking these diverse participants is a consequence of the fundamental differences in objectives of each of these institutions on the one hand and the sheer size of the petroleum industry on the other. It's true that the energy "shocks" of the 1970s have led to a more complex way to evaluate the cost of carrying out any enterprise; energy costs now often dominate project economics.

It is also true, however, that petroleum and its products are *less* scarce now than they were a decade ago. Hence the petroleum industry is doing its job well, without a need for complex linkages between institutions of different cultures. Universities provide training and are a source of employees, the government facilitates access to property and environmental protection enforcement, and the petroleum industry provides raw material for downstream economic growth.

Technology plays an important role in the petroleum industry, but is often widely shared. New ideas and concepts are disseminated among interested industrial participants in a time scale much shorter than the time it takes to implement significant projects. Most often the sizes of projects are such that the risk is shared among a number of industrial participants, further smoothing incremental technological differences in approach.

The size of the industry and its participants, therefore, coupled with the long-range nature of the investments, tends to drive the industry toward a self-contained, stand-alone culture that is less dependent upon outside technological stimulation. That is the nature of the industry today.

Moshe Lubin is President of Hampshire Instruments, Inc. He was formerly Vice President, Research and Development, Patent and License, for Standard Oil Company (Ohio).

Gillis Een is Counsellor, Technical and Scientific, at the Swedish Embassy to the United Kingdom.

Issues of Interaction

The panel discussion, therefore, dealt largely with issues of interaction between sectors at the periphery of the petroleum industry mission: research projects, personnel exchange, patents, publishing, etc., which are very important to universities, but of more modest interest to the industry.

The panel agreed on the following definitions and statements:

- Research is the generation of new knowledge and is the main concern of universities and certain government laboratories.
- Development is the use of this knowledge for the generation of new products and services, and is the main concern of industries.
- Thus, the interface between university and industry very often is identical with the interface between research and development (or science and technology, if that vocabulary is preferred).

It was useful to identify three sizes of industry, *i.e.*, small- and medium-sized industries, large industries, and very large industries.

- *Small- and medium-sized industries* tend to take no part in research. They also provide very little input into the planning of research in universities and state-operated research institutions. They are usually passive in relation to the teaching curricula of the universities. They have limited resources of their own for development, and need help in that area from time to time.
- *Large industries* tend to have their own research in areas close to their established businesses. In addition, they often support research in universities in areas adjacent to their own, thus exercising a certain influence on the planning of that research. They usually have an informal influence on the teaching curricula of the technical universities. Typically they have full resources to carry out all development work in-house, needing outside help only with more risky projects.
- *The very large industries* create their own environments. They often carry out a fair amount of research also in areas adjacent to their established businesses. They have very strong influence on the planning of research in the universities. Due to the often large-scale recruitment of people for research and development, they also have strong influence on the technical curricula of the technical universities. They have full resources to carry out all development work in-house, including the more risky projects.

Industries of all sizes wish to be flexible and adaptable regarding plans and staff. In some countries this is done by "hiring and firing" — and the US was mentioned as an example of this. Other countries — and here Sweden was mentioned as an example — have far-reaching legislation that make it virtually impossible to fire anyone. This results in a rigid organization, but flexibility can be maintained in cooperation with a university. Thus, university interaction becomes an alternative to hiring an in-house staff.

It was said that very large industries maintain flexibility by recruiting the best people and by in-house training aimed at versatility.

The largest part of the costs of teaching and research in the universities is paid by the state or federal government. There are exceptions to the rule, such as in the US. Thus, the state has a deciding influence on teaching curricula and basic research and the influence from industry is marginal.

The flow of personnel in both directions between industry and university was discussed. In some countries, there is a flow of professors to industry. In Sweden, there is a flow of professors in both directions due to the fact that salary incentive in industry is eliminated by the tax system. Prestige was mentioned as a barrier which keeps the professors in the universities in many countries.

The "Brain Drain"

Some participants had experienced "brain drain" from the universities as a result of close interaction with industry. One problem in this interaction is the stop/go mentality in small- and medium-sized industries. The university finds it difficult to cooperate on a basis which makes it the sole buffer in the system. Over time the university has to fulfill its basic tasks — to teach and to carry out basic research. Thus it is necessary to carefully balance urgency against continuity.

When it comes to publishing the results of research, there is often a conflict of interests between the two parties. This must be dealt with in the original research contract. Sometimes though, the industry has a surprisingly open and liberal attitude toward publishing: ELF Aquitaine in France was mentioned as an example of this.

From industry's point of view, there is competition with tax money over people and resources. Tax money is impersonal and tends to distort the picture and the targets.

On the other hand, government-operated research centers have a stabilizing effect on the research community and can be a refuge for ideas which are out of fashion in industry. Given the right environment and freedom of action, the results can be outstanding. The Laboratory of Molecular Biology in Cambridge, UK, with its six Nobel laureates was mentioned as an example. In a sense, this is a university department without teaching.

There is also the French Thomson Group, which has a small number of people specializing in university contacts. They do not carry out research themselves. Their experience has been a positive one.

A mixed working group from university and industry often works better than a "pure" group. The explanation may be found in the reduced internal competition, due to the differences in the two types of careers.

During the discussion, Dr. Garnier presented a case study of the pursuit of a joint university–industry program in Enhanced Oil Recovery (EOR) in France. This area was identified as a target of opportunity by industry and government officials. The problem was one of structuring an effective research program making use of the industrial, public (government), and university sectors.

Comments

The discussion of this specific case centered around the wisdom of significant government orchestration of the development of a product (microemulsions) or a technique (use in EOR) to be applied by industry in the private sector. It was pointed out that employment in the government research centers is essentially permanent. This raised the implication that, at best, this situation may lead to unimaginative approaches and, at worst, may create a built-in inefficiency in the possible answers to a problem that might ignore truly innovative solutions. Mission-oriented government research is not seen by some people as the most cost-effective solution to free market applications. Nevertheless, that system provides for long-term financial support and suitable conditions for basic research. This assumes that French industry will, indeed, receive *a* solution to carry toward application. A number of participants felt that much of the mission-oriented basic research should be carried out by the industry most interested in its commercialization.

The discussion then turned to other experiences in the petroleum industry. It was pointed out that Norway, a relative newcomer to the petroleum-producing countries, is rapidly building its research and development competence in this field through the direct involvement of industry (Shell and ELF), both in providing research staff and in training Norwegian technologists.

An additional observation was made that many successful industry–university interactions occur when the industry draws on the university for areas outside the industry's expertise; this is industry's way of keeping watch on the peripheral sciences that might have an impact on its products or services.

Various ways to facilitate industry–university interaction are being continuously developed. The group heard a description of a variant on the research park concept being developed in Houston by four universities and industry, one of the features being the integration of adjunct disciplines, such as sociology and economics, into the spectrum of research services provided by universities to their industrial clients.

It was generally felt that industry's needs could be better served by changed university curricula. Incorporation of economics training was cited as a case in point.

On the issue of commercialization of university research, patents and patent policy were not seen as important issues.

Chemicals

J. Robert Lovett

In starting this workshop, the guidance received from the conference organizers was that the panels should provide examples, draw upon personal experiences, and offer observations on country differences. I can deal with two of these broad areas of guidance, but I'd like to confess right up front that there's no way I can provide any real perspective on the third, namely, country differences.

In fact, the state of my competence in this regard reminds me of a story. When the great American humorist, Robert Benchley, was attending Harvard, he was once asked to write an essay on the treaty between the US and Great Britain covering fishing rights off Nova Scotia. Apparently this treaty led to serious discord between these two countries for many years. Benchley started this essay by saying, "Many scholars have examined this treaty from the British point of view and others have considered it from the American point of view. I intend to examine it from the perspective of the fish."

Well, like Benchley's fish, although I'm vitally interested in the outcome, at the moment I'm on the wrong end of the hook.

Until recently, when I moved to the United Kingdom and switched from R&D management to commercial management, the entirety of my real life industry–academic interface experience was gained in the US, and it would be highly presumptuous of me to imply that I have any real knowledge of the state and problems of university–industry interactions in Europe.

And so, in preparing for this meeting, I decided I could either discuss the issues that prompted the conference in a pretty shallow and uninformed way or I could focus in on my real-life experience back in the US, trying to help mobilize the chemical industry and the universities to work on the issues now facing Europe. I chose the latter approach on the basis that it would be more useful to make a presentation on administrative techniques aimed at getting industry and university opinion-formers to work together rather than a presentation by a US industrialist on European university–industry interaction—a subject about which I know precious little. If you'll bear with me, the experience I intend to focus on is my involvement in the conception, creation, and early operation of the US Council for Chemical Research (CCR).

The CCR is a nonprofit legal body, incorporated in the state of Delaware and

J. Robert Lovett is President and member of the Board of Directors, Air Products Europe, Inc., Great Britain.

comprising at last count 39 industrial and 135 university member institutions. I was privileged to be one of its founding fathers and one of its directors before moving to the UK. I'd like to briefly describe the factors leading to its formation, the roadblocks faced in creating it, and the benefits gained from its existence. I'll insert the lessons learned (by me) relating to working the university–industry interface as I go along.

As indicated, I believe these lessons, although learned in a different environment, could have relevance to anyone in Europe who wants to improve the quality of university–industry interactions so that the issues being addressed by this conference can be worked out in the most constructive fashion.

Why Was CCR Created?

I suspect all of you would agree that US chemical companies have been pretty successful. Their stock in trade and a major cause of their profitable growth during the past 40 years has been rapid, frequent, and successful product and process innovation. Most of the scientific and engineering talent that caused these innovations to occur have come from the US higher education system. In addition, quite a few but certainly not all of the fundamental science and engineering concepts from which these new products and processes flowed also came from that nation's research universities. For these reasons, it would seem reasonable to suggest that the best way to guarantee future advances in US chemical science and technology would be for US chemical companies to keep their interactions with universities strong and effective. It would seem obvious that their best interests would be served by ensuring that the chemical science and technology departments of these universities stay healthy and productive.

By the same token, the chemical engineering and chemistry departments in US universities have a great stake in the health of the US chemical industry. It is where most of their graduates find employment and it is certainly a major source of direct and, at present perhaps more important, indirect financial support. By the latter, I mean to say that the level of government support for a particular discipline tends to be at least roughly proportional to the importance that discipline is judged to have to the nation's economy and overall welfare. Industrial leaders clearly affect this judgment.

Yet, despite this obvious, mutual interdependence, by the late 1970s such a wide gulf had been created between academia and industry that many believed that university–industry interactions had, at best, become counterproductive and, at worst, had become a significant threat to the future health of the chemical industry.

The CCR was formed as a vehicle to narrow this gulf. However, it only came about after severe external threats made its need for existence obvious to just about everyone on both sides of the fence. Specifically, the perception that there would be major government cutbacks in funding of university research in the late 1970s prompted academia to turn back to industry for support; and public antagonism toward the chemical industry due to environmental issues, the severe worldwide competition in the chemical industry, and oil shocks prompted the chemical industry to realize it needed all the friends it could get and specifically it needed academia working *with* it, not against it, if it were to stay healthy. A rapprochement was mutually desired and both sides could be made to see that cooperative co-existence could be beneficial, if not essential.

● *Lesson 1. Successful marriages require both parties to recognize a need for a partnership. If someone had tried to create CCR ten years earlier, they would have failed.*

How Was CCR Created?

The way CCR was formed is also instructive. In early 1979, "Mac" Pruitt, Vice President for Dow Chemical, decided the time had come for someone to take the initiative to bring industry and academia together to discuss their problems. Therefore, under his leadership, Dow Chemical brought together at its Midland, Michigan, headquarters over 100 opinion-formers from academia and industry, along with key government personnel. The focus of this first conference was represented to be on improving communication and the flow of scientific knowledge across the industrial–academic interface. The participants, I think, wondered why we had been called together at such great expense to Dow, and the university people in particular were very suspicious of Dow's intent.

Although Mac had a clear plan in mind, he avoided overplaying his hand at this first meeting and only lightly touched the formal techniques he had in mind to work the problem.

The closest he came to tipping his hand was in showing a newly designed emblem representing the three key influences on chemical science and technology — academia, government and industry. Mac wanted to be sure none of the three were given top billing because he felt all three would have a major influence on the result. The meeting hit a responsive chord and, at its conclusion, the conferees agreed to a follow-up meeting in 1980 to further discuss the issues raised at Midland.

A Steering Committee was appointed consisting of M. Pruitt (Dow), G. Bugliarello (President of Polytechnic Institute of New York), N. Hackerman (President of Rice University), J. McKetta (The University of Texas), and myself. The Steering Committee, in turn, appointed a task force comprised of university and industrial leaders with the following charter:

● Examine objectives and current activities;
● Identify actions to further these objectives; and
● Propose action at 1980 conference.

This task force worked diligently throughout 1980 and put together a formal proposal for consideration by representatives from industry and the research universities of the country.

The Bethlehem Conference

The formal proposal that had been developed was presented to the second conference on cooperative advances in chemical science and technology, co-hosted by Air Products and Chemicals and Lehigh University, which was held in the fall of 1980 in Bethlehem, Pennsylvania. This second conference brought together department heads of chemistry and chemical engineering from 95 research universities in the US, as well as senior technical officers of 45 companies vitally interested in chemical science and technology. Chemical and chemical engineering societies, government agencies and the media were also represented. In all, 261 conferees, representing every group interested in chemical science and technology were present.

The proposal that was presented to this body envisioned forming a permanent organization of definite form and substance. The proposal was discussed in panels and workshops during the two-and-one-half day session. The objectives that emerged for the new organization were:

● Promote understanding and cooperation;
● Improve climate for innovation;
● Promote education of chemical professionals; and
● Provide new basic research funds.

The activities of the new organization were to be directed toward achieving these objectives. Membership criteria were recommended and dues proposed. A governing board and executive-director/management structure was contemplated. Annual meetings of the general membership were proposed to be held to bring together representatives of academia and industry to address a broad range of topics of mutual interest and concern. Committees were to be set up to research these topics and develop a program of action for the organization. The importance of this aspect of the initiative cannot really be over-emphasized. To my knowledge, this was the first time industrial vice presidents of research and chemistry and chemical engineering department heads had formally agreed to come together on such a grand scale to work on problems and opportunities of mutual interest. The Bethlehem conference in 1980 put it all together, and the CCR concept was well on its way to being formally accepted.

● *Lesson 2. Even when both parties to a marriage sense a need for partnership, a champion is needed to get things going. Mac Pruitt was clearly the champion for the creation of the CCR, and without his initiative and his clever political skills it is doubtful that as broad and meaningful a marriage between industry and academia in support of chemical science and technology could have occurred, despite the need.*

Road Blocks and Pitfalls

At any rate, as a result of the Midland and Bethlehem conferences, and a great deal of fancy footwork by a dozen or so dedicated industrial research VP's and university department heads, the CCR was well on the road to being launched, but there were still a great many road blocks and pitfalls that it had to get around before it could be perceived to be an ongoing and viable organization.

Perhaps the most serious pitfall was what I call the "It's everyone's problem and therefore no one's problem syndrome." Since everyone is interested in university–industry interactions, there is a tendency for everyone to want to be involved. In the case of CCR, in those early days we found quite a few different people from a host of government agencies and the major professional societies seriously wanting to be involved and/or take the problem off our hands. While we kept all of these interested people informed and listened to their suggestions, we avoided like the plague involving any of them in CCR in an official sense. We perceived — rightly, I feel — that the greatest value of the CCR was to get the most senior industrial and academic leaders together to work out their problems. I'm convinced if we had let others take over, we would have failed.

● *Lesson 3. In reconciling after a divorce, marriage counselling may have merit, but the two partners have to work out the problems on their own. The marriage counsellor can't get into bed with them.*

A second serious potential pitfall was the differing end results desired. Industry wanted an academic partner that would be supportive of its aims, ready and able to produce varying numbers of well-trained scientists and engineers at the drop of a hat and willing to turn over the fruits of its basic research to industry with no strings attached; academia, on the other hand, wanted more industrial support for its research and, moreover, they wanted this support to be totally unrestricted. If, by chance, the research led to a commercially rewarding result, they wanted to get the lion's share of the rewards; in addition, as an aside, it was interesting for me to observe that although all the professors I talked to were concerned about their students, few knew very much about what base training would best train a student for a successful industrial career — and even fewer were aware of the even more fundamental issue of how many of and what kind of student is even needed by industry.

● *Lesson 4. Perhaps the most important lesson I personally learned is that in working on industry–academic interface issues, the ability/need to compromise is very important. I was the chairman of the committee that came up with the funding approaches and formula for the Chemical Science and Engineering Fund. Every word and phrase required each side to give a few ounces of blood, and getting this agreed to was a good example of the trust-building and compromise-making required to make the CCR a viable body.*

What's Been Achieved?

These issues are not yet totally resolved (but at least they're starting to be worked out). Committees have been formed comprising university and industry leaders to deal with each of these subjects and more. There are at present eight standing committees dealing with all facets of interface and CCR governance issues. These are as follows:

CCR Standing Committees:
- Executive
- Membership
- University/Industry Interaction
- Program (for annual meeting)
- Scientific Manpower and Resources
- Government Relations
- Nominating
- Science Advisory

I'm told important progress has been made by all of these committees, and I'm sure more will be made in the years ahead.

Turning to the very important area of increased funding, in 1982, CCR's first real year of fiscal existence, a distribution of over $0.5 million was made from the central fund and three-year pledges of new industrial support totalling $10 million were recorded as a result of CCR's existence. There is every reason to believe both of these numbers will be larger in 1983 and beyond as the momentum builds for this type of support.

But I don't feel this very tangible indication of increased cooperation is the most important accomplishment derived from the CCR initiative.

The most important achievement of CCR, I feel, is the step-change increase in the level of understanding by both sides of the other's problems, needs, and opportunities. The four annual conferences attended by leading decision-makers and opinion-formers on both sides of the academic–industry interface and the activities and efforts involved in the planning of these conferences have alone provided exponential growth in the number of transactions between the industrial and academic leaders most closely involved in chemical science and technology. And each of these transactions has the potential for additional cooperation. As I see it, CCR has provided the mechanism for a useful and productive dialogue between industry and academia. What results will come from this remarriage only time will tell, but I'm confident that both the US chemical industry and the nation's university chemistry and chemical engineering departments will benefit.

In conclusion, let me summarize the lessons I feel I've learned from this exercise:

- No progress will be made unless both sides of the university–industry interface really *want* progress to be made.
- Even if both sides want to see something happen, I suspect nothing much will happen unless a champion and at least 10 but probably (initially at least) less than 20 influential opinion leaders from both sides of the interface become committed to working the problem.
- The best way to kill an initiative is to get a third party into the act whose objectives and motives are peripheral to those of the two principals. Saying it another way, the objectives and motives of the two parties to this issue, while in-

terdependent, are so far apart that a third party can only serve to make it more difficult for the two principals to really and finally get together.

- Don't be impatient and be willing to compromise. It has taken four years to get to the point where at least the most senior and the most influencial opinion-formers on both sides of the academic–industrial interface understand both sides of most of the issues involved. It will probably take four more before compromises and acceptable accommodations are reached.

And so, in summary, if you want anything real to happen in your own country on the topic of university–industry interactions, ask yourself:

- Do both sides of the interface in your country want to work the problem? And do you and they understand the problems, needs, and opportunities on both sides of the interface?
- Do you have champion(s) to work on the problem?
- Can you focus the issues cleanly enough so that progress can be made?

Overview of Policy Issues:
Panel Report on Chemicals

Fritz Fetting

The establishment of the Council for Chemical Research in the United States appears to be a rather unique arrangement. A brief survey of other countries indicates that modes of cooperation and degree of interaction between universities and industry in the chemical field vary greatly.

The research links between the chemical industry and universities in the Federal Republic of Germany are working through several channels. The most important one is the close personal communication between former students and professors and between colleagues from both sides working on various committees in different professional and business organizations.

In addition, a large number of chemists holding senior positions in industry regularly give special courses at universities. Government support has also facilitated cooperation by providing funds for research conducted jointly by a university group and its counterpart in industry.

In Japan, the personal communication channel between former students and professors is also pronounced. Consulting arrangements for professors to work with industry are another channel.

The degree to which university professors interact with industry reveals interesting country differences. In Denmark, strong anti-industry sentiment precludes most collaboration, whereas in Germany all professors of chemical engineering must come from industry. To encourage cooperation in Sweden, The Board for Technical Development (STU) gives grants for development projects where 50% is financed by industry. In Canada, professors can work full-time for industry while maintaining their university positions.

The widely acknowledged axiom that "technology transfer is accomplished through people" appears to be reflected in the personal communication network as the most prevalent mechanism of interaction between universities and industry in the field of chemicals. The fundamental science and engineering concepts needed for product and process innovation in this competitive area are likely to reinforce cooperative arrangements. This underscores the importance of each partner maintaining its technical vitality so that the resources, when combined, are mutually beneficial.

Fritz Fetting is a Professor of Chemical Technology at the Institute of Technology in Darmstadt, Federal Republic of Germany.

Mechanical Engineering

S.A.V. Swanson

This paper is written from the point of view of one of the largest departments of Mechanical Engineering in the UK, in one of the largest university institutions of science and technology in the UK, but with some knowledge of how conditions vary within the UK and between the UK and other countries.

Development of Competence

The development of competence in large part depends on education and training. General observations about the system of schooling in the UK reveal some of the major strengths and weaknesses.

Schools (for students to age 18)

The best schools in Britain give a very good understanding of mathematics and science and of other subjects, coupled with an awareness of what happens in the real world, and a sense of curiosity. But many schools are defective in one or more of these respects, and students from such schools have a bad start for their university studies.

Undergraduate Courses

Students coming from school to pursue an undergraduate degree can have little knowledge or understanding of engineering, though some may have heard enough about some kinds of scientific research to be excited by it. For engineering students to spend one year in industry between school and university is now common in the UK, but there are not enough training places in industry for all the students who might benefit. In my department, 60% to 70% of students have spent a year training in industry, most of them in companies that collaborate with the department in the planning and oversight of undergraduate courses and associated training. Students who have spent a year in training are, in general, better able to relate their analytical studies to design and manufacture. We encourage students in their

S.A.V. Swanson is Pro Rector of Imperial College, Great Britain. Formerly he was Head of the Department of Mechanical Engineering at Imperial College.

final year to work on projects which have originated in their sponsoring companies. This is good, but it requires the college staff to adapt from their more accustomed style of supervising projects which have arisen from their own research.

Postgraduate Research

More than half the people working for a Ph.D. in my department are from outside the UK, and the proportion is similar in most engineering departments in UK universities. Possible reasons for this are:

- the near-closure of the academic career route which was the traditional prospect for some Ph.D.s;
- the belief that a Ph.D. is valued in engineering industry little, if any, higher than a B.Sc.;
- the salaries offered in industry to new graduates with B.Sc. degrees, which are higher than they could hope to receive as research students or assistants.

The nature of some present-day engineering research is not well suited to the traditional method of one supervisor, one research student, and one problem. Group supervision is undoubtedly good, but it is often difficult to be sure that a particular research student has identified, analyzed and solved a problem (or brought it to a proper breaking-off point). In some fields of engineering research, there is a risk that Ph.D.s will be awarded to people who are really highly-skilled numerical analysts and computer programmers, with little idea of the wider meaning of engineering.

I observe a decline in the standard of writing in theses and other publications, and I understand that in many UK schools the use of the English language is not taught as a subject in its own right. The nature of much communication through TV and the press does not give students many good examples of the proper use of English (I think that this problem exists in other countries also). There is some evidence that the effectiveness of engineers in industry is limited by their poor abilities in communication.

Effectiveness of Mechanisms for Research Interactions

Within the field of mechanical engineering there are varied types of mechanisms for interaction involving universities and industry.

Research Councils (primarily the Science and Engineering Research Council)

This Council traditionally supported scientific research and relatively "pure" research in engineering. Good proposals have been rejected because they were not "pure" enough to satisfy the traditional criteria, but not specific enough for industry to support them with money. There are signs that things are getting better in this respect. Teaching Companies and Cooperative Awards in Science and Engineering are mechanisms which put Research Council money into work in which universities and industry collaborate.

Industry-Based Research Associations

In theory, these associations should be channels for interactions at a level of interest to the whole of one industry rather than a particular company. In practice, the functions of these research associations have been disturbed by large changes in the respective industries, some of which have declined and some of which have been re-formed into a smaller number of larger groups. They tend to be formed by established industries, and some of the most technologically advanced industries are too young to have thought about that form of collaboration.

A different form of collaboration is represented by nation-wide gatherings of university research workers who keep in close touch with the industry to which their work is related (*e.g.*, the Universities' Internal Combustion Engineering Group). This can also be an effective way of maintaining interactions.

Government Research Establishments

Some of these (*e.g.*, the National Gas Turbine Establishment) have long-term research programs which include provision for work to be done in universities.

Government Departments

Those government departments which would be expected to have a large research and development activity have their own establishments but also sponsor a lot of work in universities. The Ministry of Defence, in particular, is a very large sponsor of engineering research in universities. The work supported is remote enough from particular applications not to require a security classification, basic enough to be better done where it will not be interrupted by urgent short-term matters, but applicable to projects which are intended to be in service in the foreseeable future. Such work is usually sponsored in stages, and the discussions about the directions that successive stages should take are a good example of interaction between universities and one rather special industry.

Nationalized Industries

These included originally the public utilities (gas, electricity, coal, railways), but have more recently included others such as Rolls-Royce and British Leyland. Many of them sponsor research in universities, and this is often part of a long-term plan in which university staff have an advisory role, either informally or formally through committees. Much of the research and development work of these industries needs facilities on a scale which requires a large central organization, and the work given to universities is, therefore, a relatively small part of the whole.

Company Sponsorship

Sponsorship of research tends to come from some of the larger companies, and to be on a relatively long-term basis. The chief engineer of one company reports that he gets good value for money by paying for perhaps only one or two research assistants at any one time in one part of my department because he then has a "think tank" which knows his general future needs but is insulated from the urgent day-to-day problems.

Commercial secrecy has always been a problem, and can be a serious problem in an industry which now consists of one or two large groups who need to invest enormous sums of money in developing the next generation of their products and who naturally want to keep their ideas from their competitors.

Staff Exchanges

Industrial staff come into university engineering departments in several ways: visiting professors (usually part-time) for particular courses, technical or other staff to introduce case studies, and junior staff for two or three years to work on research in the company's field of interest. The first and the last are usually effective; the second and the third are not always as effective as we would like because time and experience are needed for visitors to contribute effectively to a course.

Academic staff do spend periods of a few months or a year in industry and benefit greatly, but this is not done as often as we would like.

Consulting Arrangements

In many mechanical engineering departments, the academic staff are free to be employed as consultants on an occasional or a continuous basis. These contacts are often a source of research ideas and sometimes of sponsored research projects.

Commercialization of University Research

Patents

Patents are a traditional way of turning ideas into saleable products. University experience with patents has been, on the whole, disappointing. Part of the reason is probably that, whether the idea is patented or not, work needs to be done in turning it into a product, and either the inventor or the licensee or both have underestimated the need for this work.

Formation of a Company

I know one or two examples where university staff have formed a company to develop an idea to the stage of making and selling the product. Sometimes the company has remained in private ownership, and sometimes it has been bought by a bigger company that was willing to pay a good price to get the product. Obviously there are limits to the extent to which university staff can share in the running of companies while still giving proper attention to their university duties.

Appendix

Research Grant and Contract Income
from the Annual Accounts of Imperial College, 1981–82.

	Imperial College	Mechanical Engineering Department
Research Councils	£6,860,571	£614,783
Government Departments	£1,170,269	£216,355
Industry and Commerce	£1,325,625	£321,202
Charities	£697,915	£1,455
Overseas	£447,218	£85,143
Others	£484,771	£40,529
Departmental Services	£625,150	
College Overheads	£745,318	
TOTAL:*	£12,356,837	£1,279,467

*This total can be compared with the total grant plus fee income for the same year of £33,565,696, of which the Mechanical Engineering share was £1,786,000. The Mechanical Engineering research income came from 95 grants (£731,508) and 131 contracts (£547,959).

Overview of Policy Issues:
Panel Report on Mechanical Engineering

Jørgen Fakstorp

Mechanical engineering faces a number of important challenges both in the shorter term and the longer perspective; this is true for mechanical engineering as an academic discipline and as an industrial endeavor. What distinguishes the present situation from many earlier ones is not so much the material and economic magnitude of these challenges as their complexity and the speed with which they will have to be addressed by industry and the academic establishment. For universities, this includes the dual role as provider of education at the highest levels and as a research and development resource of great importance and variety.

Complexity is a central characteristic of the current situation. Used in the context of challenges facing mechanical engineering, it means in particular the diversity, the high degree of interdependence, and the interdisciplinary nature of the issues involved.

A Catalogue of Issues

In these challenges there are some opportunities and a great many concerns. They have their origin in internal, intra-industrial factors, and in external societal factors as well.

Let us try to group some of the issues with the following points:

- Computer-based design and information transfer techniques (*e.g.,* CAD/CAM).
- Computer-based automation technologies in manufacturing systems (NC machine tools, PC/PSC/PLC, IC design for work stations, robotics, FMS).
- Changes in work organization and man-machine relations.
- New materials and composites in structures, products, and tools.
- Increased complexity and higher nonmaterial value content in products.
- Extreme functional requirements (stress, corrosion, temperature) of systems and components.
- Availability, low breakdown rate and easy repair requirements of complex systems.
- Process yields, reject rates, and cost and efficiency of quality control.

Jørgen Fakstorp is Vice President (retired) of F.S. Smidth & Company, A/S, Denmark.

- Environmental safety, energy conservation, product liability and similar considerations in product design and selection and in the manufacturing process.
- Commercial importance of and difficulties encountered in large overseas contracts for manufacturing plants in the form of turnkey supply.

When, how, and to what extent an engineering company should acquire any, some, or all of the new competencies necessary to deal with the items listed and make investments in equipment and plant is a business decision, not a technical question, because of the magnitude and degree of integrated involvement.

It is at present impossible to outline useful general advice and guidelines to assist in such decisions. Mechanical engineering is an immensely broad field, comprising large and small companies, old and new industries, highly localized operations, and globally active conglomerates.

Intricacies and Interrelations

To this must be added a number of contextual problems related to the rapid changes and their all-pervading character. The nature of these problems is such that they are difficult to cope with as possible subjects for university research or teaching, without rather far-reaching changes in institutional organization and division of subjects.

- The interdisciplinary communication gaps coupled with growth at the interfaces creates rapid development of highly specialized argots. Example: microcomputer designers and software specialists — who are in the center of much of the development having a radical effect on manufacturing processes in the mechanical industry — use concepts and speak and write in a language that is only understood by their own "tribe."

    However, the analysis, documentation, evaluation and presentations for general management's decisions must be prepared by mechanical engineers. Rapid diffusion of relevant knowledge is a bottleneck of considerable importance.
- The absence of determinism in many of the new technical breakthroughs has resulted in the absence of a consistent body of information about cause and effects of new technologies on company structure, employment, innovation, degree of integration of product, process and tool development, etc. The truth is that nobody knows much about the more general and longer-term consequences, and so there is a plethora of conflicting opinion. Trends and tendencies when analyzed lead to seemingly incompatible conclusions.

    The industrial decision-maker must function, based almost wholly on his own perception of a single company's particular situation, without much assistance from outside sources, established objective criteria, and empirical business research data.
- The question of whether to apply new technologies as a means of resurrecting obsolescent fields of activity or of catering to limited markets ("niches") as opposed to moving into entirely new fields — "sunrise" branches — must be dealt

with early on in a decision process and often on the basis of insufficient evidence. The decisions are of far-reaching consequences for a company's future, entail high risk, and are often irreversible.

- The high degree of integration of design, specifications, logistics, and machinery capability necessary to harvest the full benefits of the new systems requires an early sizable investment in standardization of virtually millions of inputs in a computer-adaptable form and of logical hierarchies of systems with built-in future capabilities, partially unknown.

  This requires heavy assistance of people skilled in software creation and application, areas outside the traditional competence of mechanical engineers. There is a risk of conflict at this stage, since a new overall administrative system of manufacturing may be experienced as a "black box", an external graft right in the very center of the company's capability.

- The increase in system complexity and hierarchical interdependencies, not only in products, tools, machines, or manufacturing plant, but also in supply and contracts, demands early introduction of integrated and often inflexible planning and control systems, which may be seen as attempts of "overkill." In addition, such complexity places unusual disciplinary demands on an organization and creates alienation because of the necessary inclusion of many new and nontechnical elements.

Interactions: Present and Future

While aspects of the present array of new technologies and their implications, to which the engineering industry must now rapidly accommodate, emanate from research and development carried out in university departments, it appears as if university and industry interaction will not have any great impact on the present innovation phase in company structure and culture. It appears also that re-education of technical personnel already employed will be the main avenue of adaptation to the new situation, simply because of the time factor involved.

As a result, many feel that the universities, with certain important exceptions, will serve industry and their own continuous competence development better by concentrating on the next generation of graduates and researchers, thus by-passing the role as immediate provider of results and specialists.

However, it is very important that curricula now be revised to qualify future graduates, who will have to serve industry in the 1990s and beyond in relevant new subjects and to provide them with the needed skills. Industry, in the broader sense, and not only mechanical engineering, may contribute to this revision process in the formulation of goals.

It is also timely to gear university research departments to the pertinent problems of the future, considering that skill and tool acquisition may have time horizons of several years.

Traditionally, the mechanical engineering industry has looked to universities for research assistance cooperation to some degree for the solution of special problems, but does not consider such interaction a main avenue for supplemental competence and product development. This is especially true for small- and medium-sized companies, traditionally formed, run, and staffed by people without university backgrounds. There are, however, considerable differences among various countries.

The general attitude is in contrast to some other fields in which process and product development is interrelating much more intensely with academic research. There are many reasons for the low level of research interaction in mechanical engineering, most of them rooted in tradition and in the fact that mechanical engineering is a very composite subject.

The present state is considered by many as distinctly unsatisfactory. Some people even consider that the rapid introduction of revolutionary machine tools, robotics, and computer controls of production machinery—which has caught almost everybody unaware—is indeed caused by the absence of an established pattern for long term commitment to joint university development in this field of engineering.

It is generally agreed that continued development will be much more scientifically based than has been the case, and for this and other reasons there is agreement that interactions must be intensified by all means available, directly or indirectly. Mention has been made of a number of untraditional approaches and examples are cited throughout these proceedings.

This intensification will not be a simple task. Most universities are under severe economic pressure, and this in a way makes them less attractive as cooperation partners, especially since the fruitful R&D fields will require expensive and service-demanding equipment. Most of the mechanical industry is also in deep trouble, so it is not a promising source of noncommitted funds, grants, or gifts.

The number of graduate students and post-graduate researchers in mechanical engineering has decreased, partly because of decreasing funds, partly because of the competitive pull from more prestigious research areas, but not least important is the lack of recognition that the mechanical business gives to advanced degrees. Since academic research openings have diminished, graduates prefer to go directly into industry.

The forms and types of interactions, as they exist, do not appear to be distinctly different from those in use by other branches of industry. Motivations for such interactions from the two sectors also appear similar. However, the exposure of students to practical work is cited as an especially important factor for university–industry research cooperation.

Education: Engineering and Management Science

All this being said, the primary aspect of interaction is in *education*. Industry's desire is to obtain graduates with a sound body of basic knowledge and a practical approach to design and manufacture. It is further considered quite important that graduates are able to write correct and precise language.

There is a feeling that mechanical engineering as an academic discipline has been in decline for quite some time, evidenced by the number and quality of graduates recruited into university engineering departments. However, this may really reflect a very general decline of school education in subjects relevant to higher education.

In some countries of Europe, the rapid growth in enrollment and reliable production of graduates from the nonuniversity engineering schools may also be a factor in the enrollment decline in mechanical engineering departments at the university level.

Changes in career prospects as perceived by students are also an influence. There is a preference for electronics, computer engineering, and production engineering, not to mention more remote fields. Many people from both worlds feel that the decline in mechanical engineering is supported by the fact that many innovations — important for mechanical engineering — are created by scientists and engineers from other disciplines.

There is a fairly universal shortage of good designers, and there are suggestions that some design talents are getting lost in the education system because of the emphasis of subjects requiring a high level of abstraction.

One reason for renewed interest in mechanics in the stricter sense is the advent of computer aids in the design process. The operation of such systems turns design into a more logical, analytical, and cognitive process. This opens the field for persons with more conventional academic profiles, but it will probably increase the trend of displacing designers with a more holistic, integrated and visual approach.

"Brave New World" and a Poor Relative

At the present time the so-called "flexible manufacturing systems" (FMS) are viewed as the ultimate form of automation in manufacture. Several machinery operations combined with sensors and logically programmed tool-exchange devices in a single work station are combined with program-controlled robots for positioning and short distance transfer and are further supplemented by automated guided vehicles.

The investment in such a plant is evidently heavy, but in many cases not nearly as heavy as one would expect. This, however, does not account for the gradual previous investment in man-hours completed in earlier phases of automation and standardization of design, preconditions for successful use of a fully automated plant. This investment in intellectual matter may often be of the same magnitude, or larger, than the cost of the physical plant.

The key to understanding the importance of this system is to fully grasp the concept of flexibility. This, combined with the diversity and integrated nature of the problems will then have an important impact on the contents and direction of research and teaching in the management science projects.

- Ungarbled and "noiseless" transfer of information and instruction inside the system from design all the way to assembled product eliminates tedious routine work and sources of error.
- Robots and integrated nondestructive automated quality control eliminate unpleasant, hazardous, and tiresome work elements.
- The domination of microelectronics in the manufacturing work stations economizes on labor and capital simultaneously, and introduces new trends in the international division of work in the elimination of comparative advantages of cheap manual labor.

- The manufacturing systems are applicable to a range of products, processes, and operations in an integrated way, thus making possible rapid new product or new model series introduction.

  Success depends upon the ability to utilize ranges of skills since the market no longer consists of individual products and watertight economic sectors, but of components, systems, combinations, and multisectoral interactions.
- Both upper and lower thresholds for economic utilization are quite elastic, making competitive scales radically different. Small series and batches become feasible, and the plants can be run with turn-down ratios hitherto unknown before staff layoffs become necessary.

  The short residence time of items under manufacture minimizes stocks and simplifies logistics.
- Certain skills become obsolete, and new competencies can be rapidly taught, but the scale of re-education requirements is enormous. In the 1990s it is expected that over 50% of the active population will have seen their qualifications totally or partly modified.

Paradoxically, the development in time scales, delays, cost overruns and number and severity of equipment failures in the construction and running of large turnkey installations in the mineral extractive industries, ship-building, power plant industry, and chemical process industries seem to be moving in a counterproductive direction.

Design, quality control, scheduling, infrastructure provisions, local construction, etc., are all well-known subjects, but when being put together to produce these large custom-made systems, it is as if the inner cohesion disappears, and things go wrong — and often on a large scale.

The very high capital costs associated with such projects and the fact that many of them are financed by public or semi-public bodies have created a pattern of guarantees and contract obligations that severely penalize errors, mistakes, and delays.

The engineering and managerial aspects of this type of predominantly mechanical work (no matter what is the ultimate purpose of the plant supplied) are not regularly taught, and the literature is very scanty and almost devoid of reliable empirical data. Here is a field in which we are so far from the asymptote of perfection that almost any initiative, however modest, will be seen as an important advance.

The Western industrial economy is, however, not simply a collection of supercompetitive sectors destined to expand and sub-competitive sectors destined to disappear. But internationalization of the manufacturing systems and the development of global technologies are forcing companies, universities and, indeed, nations to accommodate themselves to a disappearance of boundaries and to stress the need for cooperation on a scale unknown so far, and from the level of the smallest organization to the largest. This requires a rapid and radical change in climate and attitudes in industry as well as in the university world.

Development of Competence in a World of Rapid Technical Change

Erich Bloch

The subject of this conference session, Development of Competence in a World of Rapid Technical Change, is indeed a broad one. So broad that almost anything will fit under this umbrella. In particular, the topic of academic/industry interaction qualifies for inclusion in this paper. Another important issue is the role of the corporation in the continuing education of its professionals, a subject of increasing focus, discussion, and action.

My discussion has a US flavor and, in particular, represents an industry viewpoint. The examples are primarily from the semiconductor and computer industry sector and, obviously, from IBM. But I believe that, at least in general if not in detail, the observations well reflect other industry sectors and corporations' approaches.

Industry Changes

First, I would like to discuss some of the major changes that US industry faces. This is not meant to be an exhaustive list, but these issues are more important than others. These problems are shared by all of US industry, and exist to a greater or lesser degree in any country. Their causes range all the way from technology considerations to national and international politics.

Structural Displacement

By all measurements and observations, employment in the industrial sector is declining and employment in the service and information sector is increasing. Knowledge-based industries will be increasingly dominant. This trend is depicted in Figure 1.

Professor James Brian Quinn of Dartmouth College predicts that by 1990 US employment in manufacturing industries will have dropped to 18%, while that of the information and service industry will have increased to 62%. These are vast changes with accompanying dislocation, both on a personal and a corporate level.

World Competition

Competition, since the marketplace today is worldwide, does not know any national boundaries. This is not only true for the established classical industries, but

Erich Bloch is Vice President for Technical Personnel Development, IBM Corporation.

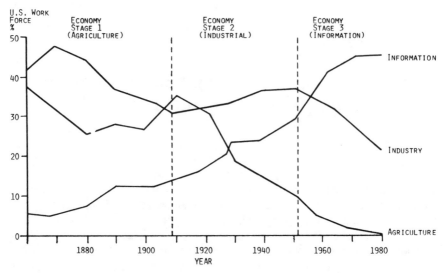

FIGURE 1. Composition of US work force. (Source: M.U. Porat. Office of Telecommunications)

equally true and even more important for high technology, leading-edge industries. The diffusion of technology, as well as the perceived need of countries to have an indigenous high technology industry, accelerates this pace. As a consequence, semiconductors are no longer primarily a US industry, but Europe and especially Japan have made major strides. A similar assessment can be made in aerospace, telecommunications, and computers.

Changes in Manufacturing

While these changes in industry are ongoing, there are other forces at work that affect the education of, and requirement for, professional technical people in industry. One such force is the change occurring in manufacturing.

Much of the economy depends heavily on the manufacturing sector. Manufacturing and the technologies it employs are undergoing a fundamental and even revolutionary change. Let me try to describe this change in historical terms (Figure 2).

The much discussed industrial revolution of the 19th century was brought about by the harnessing of power, thus leading to the consolidation of manufacturing resources and their organization into activities exploiting economies of scale. In this century, especially since World War II, we have seen and experienced further development in the manufacturing discipline, utilizing methods of batch processing, automation of individual tools, and a focus on better procedures for ordering, logistics, and control. This development benefited many companies and industries that took advantage of it.

Now we are seeing on the horizon the necessary technology to proceed in a significant way to the next step, namely, the total integration of the manufacturing

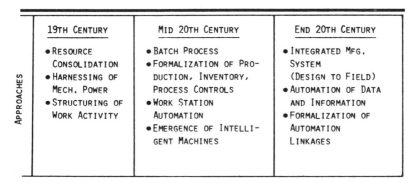

APPROACHES	19TH CENTURY	MID 20TH CENTURY	END 20TH CENTURY
	• RESOURCE CONSOLIDATION • HARNESSING OF MECH. POWER • STRUCTURING OF WORK ACTIVITY	• BATCH PROCESS • FORMALIZATION OF PRO-DUCTION, INVENTORY, PROCESS CONTROLS • WORK STATION AUTOMATION • EMERGENCE OF INTELLI-GENT MACHINES	• INTEGRATED MFG. SYSTEM (DESIGN TO FIELD) • AUTOMATION OF DATA AND INFORMATION • FORMALIZATION OF AUTOMATION LINKAGES

FIGURE 2. Phases of manufacturing.

process (from design to field support), the automation of data, and the formalization of the links between sectors of the process.

We are seeing the effect of this on the direct/indirect ratio in manufacturing employment (Figure 3), which reflects these new approaches, the impact of new technologies, and the increasing demand for technical professional people — not unlike the requirements in design and development.

In fact, the very relationship between research, development, and manufacturing is changing and becoming more intertwined and more overlapped. This change in manufacturing is driven by new technologies, such as microprocessors, computers, robots, and other new devices and tools.

Within technical disciplines, approaches are changing dramatically. Circuit design is no longer an iterative process of design and bench experimentation. Modelling and computer simulation have replaced the former approach. In addition, the

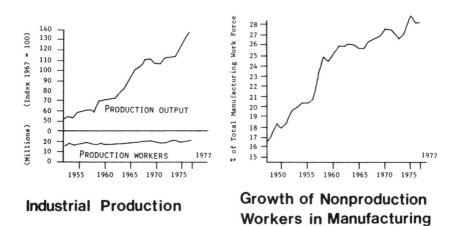

Industrial Production

Growth of Nonproduction Workers in Manufacturing

FIGURE 3. Industrial production and growth of nonproduction workers in manufacturing. (Source: Dept. of Labor and Federal Reserve Board)

criteria for optimization are changing: a few years ago, it was minimization of active elements that was the critical parameter; today it is minimization of wiring.

The conclusions I would draw are the following: manufacturing, as development in the past, is becoming more science and technology based, thus requiring more and better academically trained people. Development, design and product engineering are changing, both in terms of content and approach: new tools, new disciplines, new interactions are surfacing.

The University Connection

Sometimes these changes are caused by the results of research at universities. Sometimes, however, the universities and their educational mission are the recipients of these changes and must adapt to it.

Industry leadership is highly dependent on the use of new sophisticated technology and the attendant innovation and invention, because this leads to increasing productivity, lower cost and, in turn, higher demand. Yet we are not keeping up with the demand for professional people who are so critical to the innovation process. The example widely cited is the fact that the number of electrical engineering graduates in the US is equal to that of Japan, which has half the population of the US.

Equally important is the reduction in Ph.D. candidates. This both hurts academia and presents it with a faculty shortage. It also hurts industry, which needs their skills, learning and experience for complex technical tasks.

The Corporations and Academia

I want to consider a number of questions: First, what are the problems of academic institutions? Second, in what way can industry help?

Before I do, however, I need to comment on an observation heard at times, namely, the mistrust between industry and academia. I would characterize the relationship differently. Both sides have some insecurity about how to deal with each other; there is also the problem of inflated expectation on both sides.

Listening to university voices one gets the feeling that industry is expected to solve all problems: dollars, equipment, people. All too often, universities think that industry has an obligation to replace decreasing government funding totally and immediately. All this is unrealistic.

Industry, on the other hand, confuses research with development and is upset if university output cannot be used directly either in products or tools. Getting to a more realistic assessment of each other's role takes patience, understanding, and a realistic assessment of each other's capabilities.

The problems that academic institutions are facing, and that require industry's help, are manifold. But I would like to single out a few that, from an industry viewpoint, look like the most important ones.

First and foremost is modernization of the curriculum, the need for emphasizing new areas of education, as well as new approaches to education. The manufacturing systems engineering area is such a discipline, which needs emphasis as well as the whole area of new engineering design. These are approaches that should be taught as part of the undergraduate and graduate curriculum. With this new emphasis comes the need for the updating of equipment in academic laboratories and the need for modern services.

Faculty shortages in key areas are of great concern to industry, not just to academia. Industry must support fellowships, and help erase, at least in part, the salary differential between universities and industry; the support in terms of summer employment for faculty, as well as the loaning of adjunct professors to universities, are areas in which industry also needs to play a vital role.

By the way, the often-cited drain of faculty to industry, while real enough, is counterbalanced, at least in engineering, by a flow of people from industry to the universities. An American Association of Engineering Societies study concluded that, for the US in 1981, there were as many people leaving faculty positions for industry as there were industry people entering faculty openings in universities.

There are no universal solutions, but there are many approaches that can be tried and many different routes that can be taken.

Rather than continuing to deal with the subject in general terms, I would like to give some examples of what IBM is doing to support academia in many different ways and in many different areas. Out of these activities, I would like to highlight the following:

Grants

Many corporations are contributing to universities through the vehicle of grants and are providing both corporate funds and matching employee contributions. IBM matches its employees' gifts on a two-to-one basis.

Other general company grants are frequently free from severe restrictions and free from bureaucracy, but aimed at areas of interest to the corporation and its activities. In particular, the IBM Department Grants Program singles out departments of excellence in universities for an unrestricted yearly grant that can be used at the discretion of the department head and can be leveraged with other dollars.

Ph.D. Fellowships

The support for graduate students and their departments is an important contribution. Approximately 140 fellowships were contributed to diverse academic institutions for 1982.

Faculty

The Faculty Loan Program is a two-way street. It is the loan of an expert to a university, where the faculty does not have experience in a given field of engineering or science.

The reverse is also true. Faculty members spend sabbaticals in IBM to update their knowledge base, to work on industry problems, and many times establish through this mechanism a relationship for joint work between the academic institution and a laboratory or plant after the faculty members return to their universities.

Equipment

Another area is the Equipment Gifts Program, which makes available to universities equipment that is no longer required in the laboratories and manufacturing plants. Last year we donated approximately 1,700 tools and instruments.

Research Contracts

One of our more important interactions with universities are our research contracts. We have tripled the number of contracts in the last three years, and doubled the number of schools we have contracts with. These contracts cover a wide range of fields from acoustics to solid state and semiconductors, metallurgy, polymer science, ergonomics, application software, instrumentation.

The contract process is another example of a two-way interaction. It is administered at the laboratory department level or manufacturing department level in a direct working relationship with the researcher at the university. More often than not, the subject matter is removed from product development, even though its output leads and contributes to product development.

What about proprietary information, patent output, all the things we hear so much about? There are no hard and fast rules; we are willing to have the information find its way into the public record. This means we are selective on the content of the work we have universities do for us. We depend on the delay in the publication cycle to give us a limited-time advantage.

We are willing to have the university own the patent rights, but we expect and we want a non-exclusive use of the idea. We are flexible with regard to terms; we like to do business with universities that are flexible themselves and don't load themselves or us down with contractual complexities.

Manufacturing Systems Curricula

Very recently we announced an initiative to support academia in the development of a graduate-level manufacturing systems engineering curriculum.

What led to this initiative was our understanding of the state of manufacturing today and a conviction that the changes in manufacturing make this an important subject, worthy of academic research and teaching. IBM has announced that it will spend $50 million over the next four to five years for this initiative, $10 million for curricula development, and $40 million for computer equipment to support such curricula.

The response of academia has been gratifying. While only a small number of universities will benefit directly from this program, indirect benefits are expected, such as support from other industry sources for similar programs.

Cooperative Research

In order to cope with increasing competition in the world market, high-technology industries must increase efforts in research and development. At the same time, research tasks are becoming more complex and more capital intensive. Lead time is increasing and there are shortages of sufficiently trained manpower.

For all these reasons, some research efforts are beyond the affordability of many individual companies. The approach of the past and the present, in which each company performs its independent research, causes much overlap and duplication of effort, and is being supplemented with cooperative efforts. This is a fact in all parts of the world — Europe, Japan and increasingly in the US also. The approaches and methods are different, as are the participation and funding sources.

Cooperative research efforts in US industry are not new, in fact, they go back many years and have been primarily employed in process industries: chemistry, power generation, and paper.

In the past few years new efforts have sprung up. This time the impetus has come from a highly competitive environment, along with the realization that cooperative research is not the antithesis to product competition in the marketplace. It was also spawned by the need to support universities in an enlightened self interest. Let me mention a few of these efforts.

American Electronics Association

To help alleviate the faculty shortage, this association is asking its members to fund fellowships in science and engineering schools of their choice. The funds are forgiven if, upon graduation, the individual spends a minimum of three years on the faculty of an American academic institution.

The association also funds state-of-the-art instructional equipment through its membership.

Semiconductor Research Corporation

Another example of a new approach to industry/academia partnership is that of the not-for-profit Semiconductor Research Corporation (SRC). I would like to discuss its purpose, reasons for this undertaking, and the approach used.

The purpose of the SRC is to increase the level of basic research in semiconductor technologies. This research is aimed at both enhancing long term (five to ten years) research efforts in areas requiring a long gestation period, as well as shorter term research that will yield product results, in a three to five year time frame. It is, however, not aimed at product design.

A further purpose of the SRC is to add significantly to both the supply and quality of skilled professional people. This will be accomplished by having the research done at universities.

Another benefit will be the upgrading of the university curricula and the equipment and instruments required to do research in the various semiconductor subjects.

The participating membership of the SRC consists of over 15 corporations, not only merchant semiconductor companies, but also the major leading-edge users, such as computer companies and the makers of equipment used in the semiconductor process.

The effort will represent an expenditure of $5 million in 1982 and $11 million in 1983. This is a significant increase in research spending in this industry. For example, the NSF spends $7 million yearly for semiconductor research and DARPA about $25M.

The vehicle for university interaction is a contract either at a single-task level or at a comprehensive-center level. During the next three years, it is contemplated that numerous individual task contracts will be let and four to six major centers established (Figure 4).

Continuing or Lifelong Education

Continuing or lifelong education for technical professionals is becoming an ever more important subject. The reasons for it are obvious: shortages of professionals in key technology areas; costs of an engineer or scientist, not just in terms of salary, but in terms of the cost of support in tools and equipment; and last, but not least, the rapid development of new knowledge and technology and the resulting obsolescence factor of knowledge.

Lifelong continuing education of the scientist and the professional is, therefore, required and mandatory. This is another area where the interaction between academic institutions and industry can be highly beneficial to both partners in such an endeavor. I would like to describe the array of offerings that IBM provides for its professional population. These offerings recognize the fact that our professionals

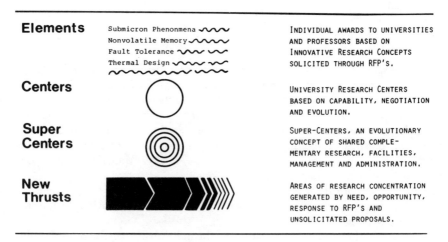

FIGURE 4. SRC program components.

come from varied disciplines, are engaged in many diverse activities or projects, and are geographically spread throughout the world.

Resident Study Program

This is a small program that allows exceptional individuals that have been in IBM's employment to study towards a Ph.D. degree in a discipline important to the knowledge base of IBM laboratories and other organizations. While pursuing such study, the individual is on full salary and all tuition and expenses are paid.

Continuing Education

This is a decentralized activity, attracting 1,500 people yearly, which allows an individual to pursue studies towards a master's degree. Courses are taught mostly by universities and colleges at the various plant and laboratory locations, partially on working time — in late afternoons and evenings. An accelerator has been added to this offering, which allows an individual, after accumulating half of the credits towards the master's degree, to return to a university or college for one semester of full-time study at full pay to complete the degree requirements.

A new requirement is that technical professionals and technical management be urged every year, in a more or less formal way, to attend a 40-hour technical course offered in IBM or at universities or in professional societies. This yearly requirement for technical education can be satisfied in many different ways and will cover many different subjects.

IBM Institute

IBM has institutes for its employees emphasizing areas of major importance. The Systems Research Institute is a ten-week computer science curriculum taught at the master's degree level. Approximately 400 people attend this institute every year.

The newly established Manufacturing Technology Institute which addresses manufacturing engineering topics is similar in structure. It is also a ten-week course with approximately the same number of people participating every year.

A third institute is the Software Engineering Institute, which is of shorter duration (two-week periods) and addresses tools and methods of software development.

I need to make a few more comments on these institutes. They are not in competition with academic offerings. They have been put in place when equivalent curricula were not available at universities. In the meantime, they have stayed and are continually charged to stay at the leading edge of knowledge and technology in these important areas. While the courses cover the subject matter in a generic way, they also highlight IBM experience, and are aimed at the purpose and requirements of the IBM environment. In order to ensure a high level of academic content, each institute has an advisory committee composed of experts from the academic community. In addition, the Systems Research Institute is accredited with the State University of New York at Binghamton and accreditation for the Manufacturing Technology Institute is being pursued.

Conclusion

The partnership of industry and academic institutions is of great importance in the competence of the engineering and science graduate and the professional in industry. This partnership can and does take many forms: gifts and grants, donation of equipment, research contracts of importance to both sponsor and institution. The efforts can be between a company and a university or can take the form of joint co-operative efforts between an industry sector and academia.

The partnership of academia and industry is a requirement, if industry, especially high technology industry, wants to remain in a leading world position. Education and quality of the professional technical resource is a necessary prerequisite for innovation — and ultimately the translation of innovation into competitive products.

Overview of Policy Issues:
Panel Report on Development of Competence in a World of Rapid Technological Change

Gordon Higginson and Torsten Lundgren

The discussion of Erich Bloch's paper naturally revolved around electrical and electronic engineers and scientists with examples and illustrations drawn from the semiconductor and computer industry, among the fastest changing fields. The change in emphasis from agriculture to engineering and then to information technology has been accompanied by a reduction in the total number of people employed, but an increase in the number of professionals. There is now a shortage of graduates in electrical engineering and computing, in industry and in university faculties.

The discussion ranged over research, first degrees, the development of professional competence, and focused especially on the maintenance of competence in established professionals.

Consideration of the respective roles of universities and industry in research brought wide agreement that the forefronts of fundamental research will remain substantially in universities, although some work is easier to handle in industry or a research institution than in a university; the development of the Josephson effect is an example. But the understanding of basic semiconductor theories can be better handled by the universities. And, of course, there is scope for cooperative research, industry-funded in the United States, but often with government involvement as in Europe and Japan. Here the question of secrecy is an issue, but its importance is often exaggerated; publication can be delayed (and is slow anyway), and research is more open than development and production.

There is criticism of university structures with their rigid divisions into specialist subjects. This militates against multidisciplinary approaches to new fields which cross the old specializations, such as systems and information engineering. It is also aggravated by the system of accreditation by professional institutions.

First degrees and initial training should have their emphasis on fundamentals over a fairly broad front, but, of course, new topics such as CAD/CAM should find their way into undergraduate studies. It is important that first degree courses

Gordon R. Higginson is Professor of Engineering at the University of Durham, and is a Member of the University Grants Committee, Great Britain.

Torsten Lundgren is affiliated with the Swedish Employers' Confederation (SAF).

should be not only a foundation for a career, but also a preparation for career-long continuing education.

The *maintenance of competence,* particularly continuing education became the major subject of discussion: what are the requirements? how should it be funded, monitored, accredited? The requirements clearly vary from subject to subject; the needs of civil engineering differ from those of electronics and computing. The system must cope with rapid change, updating individuals, and helping to keep their companies in the forefront. It must also enable some professionals to change disciplines as the pattern of professional employment changes. Updating the existing stock of professional engineers is a bigger task than keeping recent graduates up to the mark.

Plainly industry and educational establishments will both be heavily involved, but there is also an important role for the professional institutions, as has already been assumed by some, such as the IEEE in the United States, the Institute for Engineering Education in Germany and the Association for Graduate Engineers in Sweden. Funding for the most part is likely to come from the employer with a contribution from the employee.

The major part of the discussion was conducted on the tacit assumption that we all knew what *competence* was, but when we tried to define it we found the definition very elusive. Asking questions and sweeping away the cobwebs in the educational system are part of the process of maintaining competence.

Reference

Lifelong Cooperative Education, (Cambridge, MA: MIT Department of Electrical Engineering and Computer Science, 1982).

Functions of Research Institutes

Johannes Moe

Applied research is carried out in universities, research institutes, and industry. Each of these different types of institutions which conduct research has certain specific characteristics. This paper focuses on research carried out in contract research institutes.

Contract research institutes are often needed as a supplement to universities and industrial laboratories. They command a pool of competence that can be used flexibly by individual customers according to varying needs. This may be of special value to small- and medium-sized companies that have at best only small in-house research capabilities. The institutes often possess expensive and specialized research facilities that can only be efficiently operated as common resources for groups of industries. As a consequence of their dependence on the market, research institutes are generally operated more as commercial service institutions than are universities with their numerous and generally highly autonomous departments and faculty individuals.

There are, on the other hand, disadvantages associated with the concentration of resources in independent research institutes. Those institutes that are most successful in serving the short-term needs of industry are usually highly dependent upon income generated by industry-sponsored contracts, and may lack necessary resources for more long-term research. Such institutes may run the risk of obsolescence. On the other hand there is a risk that institutes that benefit from rich endowments (from governments or other sources) may become too far removed from practical cooperation with industry, even if they become first-rate scientific institutions. Hence, their contribution to the development of industry may be too limited.

Close Links Between Industry and Research Institutes

In Norway there is a relatively well-developed system of research institutes. About one-third of the total industrial research of Norway is carried out in such laborato-

Johannes Moe is Managing Director of the Foundation for Scientific and Industrial Research at the Norwegian Institute of Technology (SINTEF).

Applied Industrial R & D (1978)	Man Years		Value	
	Number	**%**	**Mill NOK**	**%**
Industrial Laboratories	4.260	67 %	929	67 %
Institute Research	2,130	33 %	465	33 %
SUM	6.390		1.394	

FIGURE 1. Industrial research in Norway.

ries (see Figure 1).

The Norwegian research institutes are strongly oriented towards commercial contract research for industry and government. On the average, approximately two-thirds of their income comes from these sources.

There is a pronounced political desire in Norway to develop closer interaction between research institutes and the universities. There are several reasons for this drive. Industry-oriented research institutes need a continuous flow of new scientific knowledge from universities in order to maintain and develop properly their scientific standards. The staff of an institute also needs the challenges and benefits from close interaction with academics in a university, as well as from interaction with the continuous stream of new student generations with up-to-date knowledge in basic subjects.

One of the major objectives of a research institute should be to serve as a training ground for future research staff and other highly qualified personnel in industry. This is most efficiently achieved if the research institute is operating in a university environment where newly graduated students are a major source of recruitment.

There are mutual benefits to be shared by employees of both parties in a cooperative arrangement between a university and a contract research institute. This mode of operation helps to assure the development of relevant educational programs. The university may hire employees of the research institute as part-time teachers in specialized topics or as advisers to graduate students during their thesis work, thus increasing the scope of teaching programs at marginal costs. Students' thesis work may also yield significant contributions to the more basic research activities within a research institute. On the national scene, the competence of university faculty may be used more efficiently to the benefit of the development of the society, through their participation in the solution of practical problems that the research institutes are addressing.

It is my view that contract research institutes of the kind described in this paper should, indeed, as a rule, be part of an environment dedicated to education in some way or other. A notable exception would be institutes which are significantly involved in classified defense research.

The NTH/SINTEF Model

There are many possible modes of cooperation between research institutes and universities. No specific solution is universally applicable. There are also many pitfalls to get around in the efforts to create and maintain such modes of cooperation. The very autonomy of the traditional European university — which is a precious asset — is one of the stumbling blocks. This autonomy is usually preserved by each research group and even by each individual scientist at a university. It may, therefore, become practically impossible to make general agreements between universities and research institutes which commit manpower resources of the university in cooperative efforts.

The cooperation between the Norwegian Institute of Technology (NTH) and The Foundation for Industrial and Technical Research at the Norwegian Institute of Technology — SINTEF — is an example of how scientific resources of the university can be pooled together with those of a contract research institute for the pursuit of practical goals in society. NTH, founded in 1910 as a government institution, is the only technical university in Norway. NTH, with its 1,500 employees and 5,000 students, covers all relevant fields of engineering in Norway as well as architecture.

SINTEF was founded in 1950 by NTH's Senate and with substantial support from industry and commerce. Originally it was thought that SINTEF should act mainly as a liaison office, taking care of the business administration side of possible contracts between university departments and individual industrial companies and the like. Very soon, however, it became obvious that there was really very little surplus manpower available within NTH, even if the intellectual potential was very significant. It was, therefore, decided that SINTEF should also employ scientific and assisting personnel, thus in effect adding to the staff of NTH.

The mode of cooperation between NTH and SINTEF is illustrated in Figure 2. The activities of SINTEF are located on the NTH-campus. The staffs of both of these institutions normally share laboratories and other facilities. Quite often they also have joint leadership within different disciplines, and there is then a frequent exchange of manpower resources.

SINTEF's goal is to perform contract research for industry, government and local authorities, and other clients, and to strengthen the interaction between NTH and society at large. The number of employees has increased continuously during the years, as Figure 3 illustrates. At the end of 1982 the total number of employees was about 1,100, of which really 60% were academics. SINTEF had a total income of 360 million NOK in 1982. About 45% of this came from contract research for industry and 25% from contract research for public authorities while the remaining

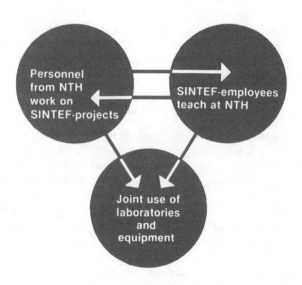

FIGURE 2. The cooperation between NTH and SINTEF.

25% was obtained as project support from the Royal Norwegian Council for Scientific and Technical Research (NTNF) (see Figure 4).

SINTEF is an independent not-for-profit foundation. It is closely tied to NTH through its aims and functions, but it is economically and administratively independent of the university.

Wide Range of Activities

The range of SINTEF's activities covers a wide field, strongly dominated by technology, but with increasing involvement in social issues, especially those concerning work environment, industrial social relations and similar areas. In 1982, the main areas of activity were the following (see Figure 5):

> Chemistry, metallurgy and petroleum technology
> Automation and data processing
> Electronics, acoustics and physics
> Civil and structural engineering
> Machine design and production engineering
> Hydrodynamics

SINTEF's organization, as depicted in Figure 6, is strongly influenced by the mode of cooperation with NTH. To a large extent SINTEF is organized according

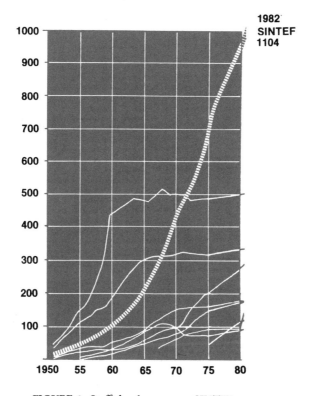

FIGURE 3. Staff development at SINTEF.

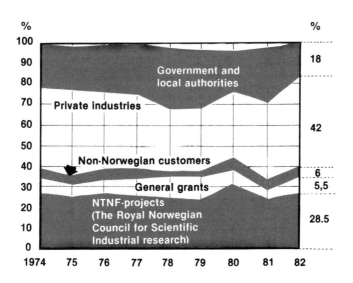

FIGURE 4. SINTEF's income sources.

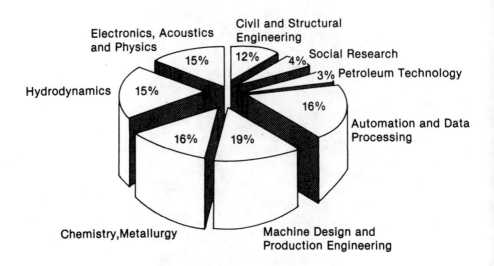

FIGURE 5. Main fields of research activities.

to disciplines in order to match the NTH groups.

SINTEF is governed by a board and a council. The board has six members, of which two are appointed by employees, while the other four are elected by the council. Of those four, two are elected among NTH faculty, and the other two externally. The board has, broadly speaking, the same authority as that of a private corporation.

SINTEF's council consists of 17 nominated and elected members and eight ex-officio members. The Rector of NTH, the Deputy Rector, and the acting chairmen of the boards of SINTEF's affiliated institutes are ex-officio members. Of the total number of 25 members approximately 50% will normally be NTH staff. The Rector of NTH is chairman of the council.

In addition to NTH's representation on the board and the council, this institution has a strong influence on SINTEF's activities through the participation of its staff in steering functions at the division level of SINTEF. SINTEF is a decentralized organization. The day-to-day management of the research activities is delegated to the individual groups and divisions.

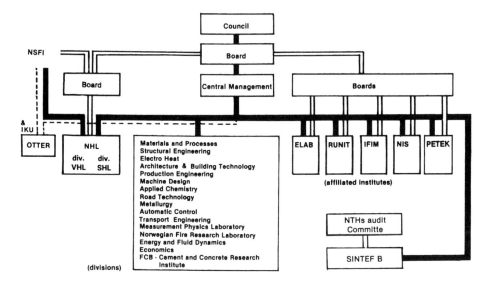

FIGURE 6. SINTEF's organization.

The close cooperation between NTH and SINTEF ensures quite efficient utilization of resources in terms of buildings, scientific instruments, and other resources. The high concentration of technical expertise contributes to high professional standards and robustness against rapid drainage of competence in periods of high demand for technical expertise. NTH/SINTEF is the dominant center of technological education and research and development in Norway.

To maintain a successful cooperation between NTH and SINTEF, it is necessary to maintain open communication between the parties on all levels, preferably joint leadership of research activities and reciprocal arrangements of part-time employment of personnel. The ability to practice day-to-day cooperation in such a way that a sense of mutual benefit is felt by each of the two parties, down to the level of every research and teaching group, is vital. No formal organization can guarantee success in this respect. Sufficient overlap in fields of activity and a level of competence to insure motivation for professional cooperation is a requirement.

Ability and motivation on behalf of the research institute to contribute in various and flexible ways to the solution of problems that the university—due to its status as government institution—cannot handle by itself is important to the university and, hence, stimulates its incentive to participate in SINTEF's contract research.

Of special concern to some customers could be the ability of a research institute working in a university environment to handle confidential information obtained from customers, as well as confidential results of sponsored projects. In our practice we have not found this to be a difficult problem. Research with top secrecy requirements, such as those related to defense research, may have adverse effects upon open interaction with the university and hence, as a rule, are avoided. Further information about the NTH/SINTEF model of cooperation can be found in references 1 and 2.

Threats Towards Harmonious Cooperation

In the cooperation between a university and a research institute there may, of course, be conflicts of interest between the two parties from time to time. The research institute must be precautious and not allow its more flexible and commercial way of operation to lead to a domination over the less firmly coordinated university system, either in its daily life on the campus or on the national scene. It is important for the research institute to play the role of a tool for the improvement of the communication and cooperation between university faculty and society at large, and not as a barrier.

In times of high demand for technical expertise, it may be more profitable for individual faculty members to sell their services directly to the external customers than through the research institute. This will have a disintegrating effect upon research teams, which hampers the development of strong research units. Large differences in salaries and other working conditions between those employed by the university and those of the research institute are similarly detrimental to the motivation for cooperation, especially if such differences lead to a drainage of qualified people away from the university and into the research institute.

Future Trends

In several industrial countries efforts are being made to develop stronger links between universities and research institutes. In Norway there is, as already mentioned, a strong political desire to establish closer contacts between the other universities and research institutes in their vicinity. The assumption is that research institutes which have succeeded in this effort will have the greatest chance of staying in the forefront of science and technology.

In this process it is important to maintain the autonomy of universities. This is not only a question of formal status, it is even more a question of the command of sufficient resources for its free research. The ability of the university to respond to the demands from society at large for relevance and constructive contribution to its development will have a significant effect upon the resources made available for university research. To meet these needs of society, universities must organize themselves internally for a more coordinated utilization of their resources. Autonomy of universities, as such, may, therefore, have to be won partially at the cost of the autonomy of each individual of its staff.

References

1. Moe, J. and Stenstadvold, K., "SINTEF—25 Years of Contract Research at a Technical University," paper presented at the Third International Congress of the European Society for Engineering Education, Lausanne, September 1975; published in the European Journal of Engineering Education, Volume 1, no. 2 (Spring 1976) (SINTEF report STF01 A76001, April 1976).
2. Moe, J. and Stenstadvold, K., "Large-Scale Cooperation Between Industry and a University Through Contract Research," paper presented at OECD's Special Topic Workshop in Paris, April 1980 (SINTEF report STF01 A80013, November 1980).

Overview of Policy Issues: Panel Report on the Functions of Non-University Research Institutes in National R&D and Innovation Systems and the Contributions of Universities

Helmar Krupp

Universities are elements of national R&D and innovation systems, which comprise a great variety of customers and suppliers of R&D and innovation-related functions. We must understand the working of such national R&D and innovation systems as a whole in order to be able to specify the role and the future potential of universities as a part.

The following is thus a description of a suitable framework with a few examples to illustrate its usefulness.

Customers for R&D

First of all, let us ask: To whom are research results addressed? who receives, uses or diffuses them? who articulates and organizes demand for R&D? who pays for it?

The principal customers for R&D are listed below:

- *peer groups in the academic world.* They are by far the predominant customers of universities. They set the standards of university research.
- *government.* This subset comprises a wide variety of governmental departments and agencies, ranging from the more traditional ministries such as those of education, research, technology, trade, and commerce to more modern ones such as nuclear power, space, armanents, and so forth.
- *sectors of industry,* such as mechanical or electrical engineering, electronics, chemicals, iron and steel, watchmakers, etc.;
- *groups of companies interested in a common subject,* maybe of generic technologies (*e.g.,* microelectronics for watchmakers, controls for machine tools);
- *individual companies;*
- *trade unions;* and
- *single-issue citizen groups* interested in, for example, the protection of the environment or product safety.

Helmar Krupp is Director of the Institute for Systems Analysis and Innovation Research, Federal Republic of Germany.

This list is probably not complete, but it may serve to illustrate the wide range of customers for R&D output, and it may help in the assessment of their demand for the services of universities.

Typology of Research and Innovation Performance

R&D performance may be classified as follows:

- *basic or fundamental research, mainly or almost exclusively addressed to and oriented by peer groups (knowledge for knowledge's sake);*

- *long term application-oriented research. Very often this is put in the same basket as basic or fundamental research. The differentiation between the two proposed here is essential, at least for two reasons:*

  — It improves the international compatibility of R&D statistics. Without this distinction, large variations of the amount of basic or fundamental research as a proportion of all R&D between countries (*e.g.,* Japan and the U.S.) or between otherwise comparable companies (*e.g.,* Siemens and General Electric) cannot be explained. If this distinction is kept in mind, the wide international variations will be reduced, and it will be found that the percentage of true basic or fundamental research even in big research-intensive companies will hardly ever exceed 1%.

  —The direction and supervision appropriate to basic or fundamental research (great freedom and informality) is not appropriate to application-oriented research, even if its targets are long-term ones. In this case, stricter industry-type management is more effective, at least from a cost and time perspective.

- *shorter-term application-oriented research; and*
- *development (including the construction and testing of laboratory prototypes).*

Further innovation-related performances include:

- *design, and*
- *testing of prototypes in factories, etc.*

In addition to this more conventional classification, there are categories such as

- *exploratory research;*
- *application development, i.e., R&D required to apply research results or a prototype to a particular task;*
- *literature research;*
- *consultancy; and*
- *composition of an expertise, etc.*

Other Criteria

There are criteria used to describe the functioning of the R&D and innovation system of a country or internationally:

- *big versus small nations:*
  Big nations can afford a large variety of well-differentiated mono-goal research institutions, whereas in a small country quite different functions are being performed within one and the same multi-goal institution (*e.g.*, TNO in the Netherlands).
- *big companies versus medium-sized companies as customers:*
  In general, universities may do well with the former, but not with the latter.
- *technology generation versus technology diffusion:*
  Generally speaking, universities should keep to the former and leave the latter to non-university institutions.
- *big versus small technologies:*
  In general, universities will not be capable to handle the former.

The German R&D System as an Example

With these classifications in mind, let us discuss the German R&D and innovation system as shown in Figure 1.

On the abscissa, we differentiate between, on the one hand, publicly supported and, on the other hand, private R&D institutions.

- *In the first category, we have the universities, the big government laboratories concentrated on atomic energy, reactor safety, environmental protection, medicine, etc., and the Max-Planck-Gesellschaft of basic research.*

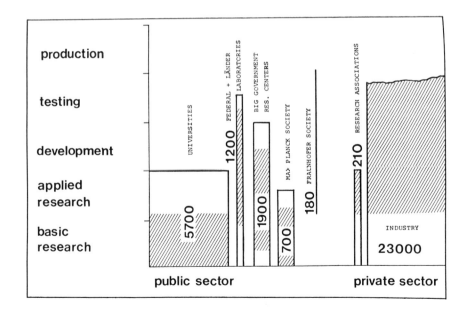

FIGURE 1. German research system (1983).

- *There we have also a variety of smaller institutions rendering public services in areas, such as testing, safety control, measuring standards, etc.*
- *At the private end, we find the laboratories of industry, and private contract research and engineering companies.*
- *Between the public and the private sectors of R&D, we find the research associations and contract research of the Fraunhofer Society, which receives some 30% to 50% of basic public support.*

On the abscissa, we have marked the different categories of performance: basic research, application-oriented research, development, testing and so forth, that leads to manufacturing of a particular product.

Within this coordinate system, we have entered the various research institutions enumerated above. The area of the different boxes is proportional to their annual budget. Between 1979 and now the absolute size of the boxes has changed, but their relative sizes (relative budgets) have not changed significantly. The shading indicates their main performance. When going from left to right, the shading is shifting upward towards development and testing, and inversely, to a more basic orientation when we proceed to the left. This leaves the institutions in the center, mainly research associations and contract research, with the task of technology transfer from bottom left to top right or, in other words, from research towards application.

National R&D and Innovation Systems

Countries differ as to

- *the proportion of public versus private funds (e.g., small in Japan, large in France and in the US);*
- *the absolute volume of the budgets. The predominance of the US disappears, if we subtract the public funds devoted to armaments (presently 70%) from the total, and countries such as the Federal Republic of Germany and Japan then compare favorably with the US;*
- *the differentiation of goals within the institutional typology. Thus, US universities are being asked to perform a much greater variety of functions than European ones, because in the US equivalents to the Max-Planck-Gesellschaft and the German research association, the Fraunhofer Society, are lacking. Since many of these institutes are and have to be interdisciplinary and the development of efficient interdisciplinary teams requires much time, the US approach may be less efficient, all the more so since the various tasks given to the US universities tend to change quite often.*

National R&D systems are highly complex and quite different, since they have evolved historically in the absence of a common master plan. Still, the above typology may prove to be a useful guide in order to understand differences, specificities and commonalities.

It is within such national contexts that universities are performing their various functions. The quality, efficacy, and efficiency of national systems differ to the extent that they develop fruitful interfaces between the various elements of the system, because it is most often at interfaces of disciplines and institutions that innovations occur.

Let me conclude by a few statements which are supposed to demonstrate the usefulness of the above conceptual framework.

● *The task of research associations is among the hardest. Therefore, it is not surprising that their quality varies widely, nationally and internationally. So, on the one hand, the German Watch Institute was unable to prepare the German watchmakers in time for the microelectronics age. On the other hand, PERA in Great Britain and the German Foundry Institute seem to be widely acknowledged as quite successful.*

● Contract research *is a very versatile instrument to help industry to adapt to structural change. Thus, it is helping German small- and medium-sized companies to cope with microelectronics and to master new generic technologies in such areas as materials, controls, and automation. With those important functions in mind, the German government is awarding small and medium-sized companies a special grant if they sponsor contract research projects in outside institutions.*

● *Classically, R&D institutions are tied to government and industry as their primary customers. With the growing importance of single-issue citizen groups, a new category of customers for R&D has arisen. Accordingly, small private institutes are being formed like the Öko-Institut in Freiburg in Germany, which specializes in environmental protection.*

● *After the last war, trade unions have formed their own research establishments in order to improve their bargaining positions with respect to industry and government. Thus, the WSI (Wirtschafts-und Sozial-Wissenschaftliches Institut Des Deutschen Gewerkschaftsbundes Gmbh) in Cologne and the staff of the IGM (Industrie Gewerkschaft Metall für die BRD) in Frankfurt are carrying out appropriate social research to serve their respective unions. It may be interesting to note that the University of Bochum has a general contract with the German Confederation of Trade Unions in the framework of which union-oriented research is being carried out.*

● *Because of its relative independence, a main function of the university may be its ability to shape new models of future societies, ignoring present contingencies and partisan interests. Such models may suffer from a lack of reality. Yet, such visions may provide stimuli to policymakers. New types of energy policies, better protection of the environment and users of industrial products, more cost-effective prevention of diseases, policies for the reduction of the consumption of cigarettes, alcohol, pharmaceuticals, and TV are not vigorously pursued by the present national governments. Here, universities may play pioneering roles in information and motivation. But, it is their remoteness from the differentiated contingencies of our societies and their lack of management which hinder universities from performing this function well so far.*

This paper is an attempt to outline the rich complexity of our research and innovation systems so that a more detailed discussion of the contribution of universities may ensue. When doing this, we will find out that the R&D functions of universities are in the bottom left corner of Figure 1. If we ask universities to serve functions higher up along the ordinate, where industry-type management is essential, then they are overburdened and inefficient.

All R&D institutions are somewhere on a scale, whose one extreme is 100% public support with the danger of ivory towers' remoteness, and the other extreme is that of 100% industry support with the resultant streamlining in accordance with purely commercial interests. Universities may increase their overall role in society by symbiosis with other elements of the R&D and innovation systems between these extremes and synergistic effects may ensue.

Overview of Policy Issues: Panel Report on the Role of Middle-Level Research in the R&D Systems

Helmar Krupp and Bjorn Englund

In most industrialized countries there is a spectrum of R&D activities, one which spans the field from basic research to development for problem-solving. The research end is characterized by long-term exploration of scientific possibilities with high risk in the market place and the development end by low risk, short-term satisfaction of urgent needs. In between those extremes, there are other R&D activities to assure the continuity that is the requisite for an effective industrial R&D system in a highly competitive market. Without supporting the theory of an innovation chain, there is much evidence of the importance of medium risk, medium-term R&D with mixed incentives. Innovations and technology transfer, emanating from basic or applied research, are likely to suffer unless there is a middle level of research activity, which constitutes an intermediary between the internationally open basic research society and the closed groups of development in individual companies. Here is the true niche for industrial research institutes.

Due to historical, political and/or organizational reasons middle level research is performed by various actors in different countries. Where the universities work under liberal regulations, as in the United States, academic research can be extended to cover middle-level research on an industry-sponsored basis. In other countries, as in Western Germany, industries realize their independence upon middle-level research, and so have grouped together to set up cooperative research institutes.

Some national governments were provident and created early middle-level research institutes to serve their industries, as in Finland. Very often a middle-level research institute originated from the activities of an individual person who was strongly dedicated to the role of technology for industrial development. That is true for TNO in the Netherlands. Regardless of its previous history and actual organization, middle-level research is today heavily subsidized by the government in most industrialized countries.

Helmar Krupp is Director of the Institute for Systems Analysis and Innovation Research, Federal Republic of Germany.

Bjorn Englund is Head of a Section in the Planning Department at the National Swedish Board for Technical Development, Stockholm, Sweden.

Functions of the Institute

Even if the idea of research institutes may be questioned from an organizational aspect, there is a reasonable consensus about the need for middle-level research. Within a compilation of the activities composing the concept of middle-level research, the following would be found:

- technical medium-term research
- pooling of technical expertise
- joint operation of specialized and expensive research facilities
- technology transfer
- training of R&D personnel

Institutes outside the university system are said to pay more attention to the applicability of their R&D results. This is quite natural, since normally they are placed in a recognizable commercial environment. The value of the output to the sponsors in terms of new knowledge must match the input in grants from sponsors. That is obvious when the institutes serve the immediate or short-term needs of their customers in accomplishing research contracts, but it is equally true in executing a cooperative research program.

One good reason for a company to sponsor a middle-level research institute is the option of easy access to very competent and highly qualified research groups. Every now and then the company runs into problems requiring a high-technology skill for their solution. It is often less expensive and more expeditious to buy prompt access to external groups of experts than to recruit and support internal ones that may not be needed again.

The same arguments can be used when very specialized scientific equipment and other expensive facilities are allocated to an institute for middle-level research. There are, for example, companies in an industrial sector using their institutes as the testing grounds for all new research apparatus entering the market.

Technology transfer ought to be a main task in middle-level research activities. Inasmuch as each research institute is a minor producer of research results compared to what is available on the global market, its own results must be associated with other knowledge. But it is easier said than done. Technology transfer has to combine R&D capabilities and scientific and technical cooperation with the outside world and technical salesmanship. One of the difficulties in achieving the optimal amount of technology transfer is the opinion among scientists that research has a higher professional status than commerce. The Japanese strategy during the first decades after World War II is still a very interesting model. In spite of the potential profitability, effective promotion of technology influx is very rare even in market economies. Many middle-level research institutes are well apt to undertake international state-of-the-art multiclient studies.

Various national programs to further technical development in small- and medium-sized enterprises engage middle-level research institutes as transmitters for new technologies. These must be adapted to small-scale production and restricted resources in skilled personnel, equipment, and funds.

Irrespective of it being a declared policy of the program performed, there is always an educational and training effect of middle-level research. Sometimes the creation of personnel competence is the sole objective for a selected program. The industrial approach in research is a valuable experience for a talented person aiming at a career in company R&D. Recruitment of key persons from a successfully finished project is unsurpassed as a way of ensuring transfer of results to a company. That explains why a prime indicator of a healthy middle-level research organization is an annual turnover of researchers on the order of 10% or more.

The Place of Research Institutes

High-risk, long-term basic research suits universities since they want to preserve their independence and they can depend on public funding. The two main functions for universities, basic research and higher education, also strengthen their claim on the public purse.

Low-risk, short-term technical development within big individual companies is often the main concern for internal R&D resources, because it is necessary to protect the competitiveness of the current range of products.

Medium-risk, medium-term research may well be allotted to specialized institutes attuned to the specific demands summarized above. Institutes are not troubled by other commitments, and so are free to put all efforts into middle-level research, hopefully bridging the gap between university and industry. They are in a position to choose the best staff, to structure the work and to adopt a strategy for these objectives. Whereas universities are discipline-oriented, the institutes can be problem-oriented and their work interdisciplinary.

There are threats against a good future for a middle-level research institute, the most important being too strong a tie with a declining industry sector. It can be fended off by a research program directed towards a properly balanced mix of customers from a range of industry sectors. Such a strategy avoids the most common criticism that a middle-level research institute has a conserving influence on an outdated industrial structure.

The Role of Universities in Economic Development: National, Regional, and International

Valentin von Massow

The Issues

● *Is it possible to ascertain the influences of universities on economic development?*

Suggestion A: The effects of university research on economic development are obvious.

Suggestion B: It is difficult to prove, in retrospect, the effects of university research on past economic development and even more difficult to forecast what effects these activities will have on future economic development. There are several points to consider.

— We can all cite impressive examples showing how university research has spawned completely new industrial developments. The most famous example is that of the establishment of the chemical industry.
— Whether university research has had, or will have any effect at all on economic development, and whether individual effects, if any, are advantageous or disadvantageous, can often be determined only after a long period of time. It is very difficult to measure such effects in detail and to forecast the effects on future economic development.
— In basic research, which is connected with broad sectors of university research, it is more difficult to establish the direct and indirect effects of research results on economic development than in the case of applied research.
— If it is difficult to realize the effects of individual projects or fields of research, then it is all the more difficult to establish the effects of the total sum of research carried out by any one university.
— At any rate, a university may imply considerable financial burden on the region in which it is located. The funds required for running a university are consequently not available for other projects in the region (specific university infrastructural costs).

Valentin von Massow is Head of the Science Policy and Promotion of Research Division in the Federal Ministry of Education and Science, Federal Republic of Germany.

Conclusion: In principle we are convinced that university research has an effect on economic development; it is, however, difficult to identify past effects and to forecast future ones as well as to make a cost-effectiveness analysis. Our efforts in this respect are often only partly successful.

Consequently, the *question* is: Can we improve the tools for measuring the effects of universities on economic development?

● *To what extent does the university aim to promote economic development?*

Suggestion A: Universities are primarily institutions providing training and satisfying the desires for scientific knowledge. The furtherance of economic development is at most a secondary task, a by-product.

Suggestion B: The furtherance of economic development has been, and remains, a declared goal of many university administrations.

The first suggestion is confirmed by the self-image of many eminent European universities. The desire for knowledge and the provision of qualified training are the primary goals. All other aims can be realized on this basis alone and are achieved, so to speak, as a natural consequence.

There are several examples of the second suggestion that economic development is a declared goal of many university administrations.

— technical institutes, which were established in large numbers in Europe during the 19th century as contributors to economic growth;
— universities oriented to special sectors of the economy, such as agricultural institutions;
— the intensive development of university subjects oriented to branches of the economy (*i.e.*, chemistry);
— land grant colleges in the United States; and
— the systematic founding of new universities in the 20th century (*e.g.*, in Finland, Portugal, Great Britain, and the Federal Republic of Germany). Admittedly, in many cases the promotion of economic development was not considered a direct goal; the idea was rather that improved facilities in a region would also strengthen its economy.

Conclusion: In general, it can be said that nowadays more emphasis is placed on the university's task of contributing towards economic development. This observation poses the question: Are the universities properly equipped and appropriately structured to fulfill this task?

● *Does one have to take new measures in order to develop the role of universities in economic development?*

Suggestion A: Many universities and sectors of university research make an excellent contribution towards economic development. No attempt should be made to control or to impede their efforts.

Suggestion B: If universities are to contribute more towards economic development, then new priorities must be established for their work and new methods must be devised for technology transfer.

Several good illustrations in support of the first proposition are to be found not only in my own country, but in many other countries, too. Particularly in the technical sectors of industry and in technical universities, research has the primary goal of producing new materials, of preparing new goods and production processes or of improving existing techniques. Contacts between universities and industry are so close that technology transfer does not cause any problems. A brisk exchange of personnel is taking place. Many bigger firms engage in research themselves. Thus their researchers can be qualified partners of those engaged in university research.

In this connection, the government should provide good basic equipment for the universities. There should be as little government intervention as possible in the way of administrative regulations or other impeding measures.

On the other hand, there are obviously some gaps and shortcomings:

— On the side of industry, the small- and medium-sized enterprises, in particular, do not themselves carry out research and development on a large scale, and often do not even employ university graduates.
— In the universities, on the other hand, there is probably still a considerable unused potential, which could be put to good use for the purpose of economic development, including those disciplines which are not directly application-oriented.

Conclusion: Problems are encountered chiefly:

— on the university side, in those subjects in which cooperation with industry and understanding of industry's problems was rare, and in which thought was seldom given to the interaction of university's activities with economic development;
— in industry, in the sector of small- and medium-sized enterprises. These enterprises lack staff who are qualified to examine whether research results are suitable for immediate use in their firm. It is also difficult for such firms to find out how science can perhaps help to solve their own problems. Often, it is impossible for them to define their problem in terms of a scientific task.

The *question* is therefore: What is being done in order to improve the contribution of the universities, particularly with regard to the economic development of small- and medium-sized enterprises?

● *Approach toward achieving improvements within the national framework.*

It is perhaps useful for the purposes of our discussion to look at several typical approaches introduced in individual countries with the aim of shaping the role played by universities in economic development more effectively. The following examples are not intended to be exhaustive, but have been selected on account of their diversity. For the most part, they have been chosen from the work done by the OECD Ad Hoc Group on University Research.

— *The establishment of new enterprises and technical colleges in poorly developed peripheral regions.* Let us take for example, the newly-established higher education institutions in the northern and eastern regions of Finland. Both of them concern themselves directly with regional planning, including planning at a community level. This approach is holistic, *i.e.*, efforts are oriented to the development of the entire region in question;

— *with aim of getting more personnel.* For example, the new Regional Technical Colleges in Ireland, particularly the National Institutes for Higher Education in Limerick and Dublin, which have been set up to reverse the lack of skilled technicians and engineers;

— *in industrial areas where the structure requires modernization.* The Ruhr University of Bochum is an example. Here the regional structure is already established and developed, but it is hoped that the university will come up with new ideas for innovations.

But as we all know, university–industry interactions are not a one-way street. Since the early 1970s in the Stavanger region in Norway, the booming petroleum industry created a demand for a new infrastructure of research facilities and institutions for higher education. In 1973 the Rogalund Research Center was founded. The regional college founded in 1969 may be a basis for creating a technical university in the future.

To Promote Regional Development

There is also increased emphasis on the task of existing universities to promote the development of a specific region; the University of Quebec, Canada, is an interesting example in this context. The University of Quebec, itself decentralized, has colleges and institutes located throughout the province. This decentralization facilitates access to the surrounding community. It is particularly useful in enabling the university campuses to offer administrative and marketing assistance to small- and medium-sized enterprises.

Another example is the coordination of applied research in the Rhone-Alpes region of Southern France and, at the same time, concentration of specific innovation-oriented fields, like microelectronics. In this connection, one should also mention, however, the efforts underway to let universities cooperate increasingly with the regions in which they are located. In my country, this is illustrated by a government-promoted pilot project being carried out at Tübingen University.

The systematic promotion of the establishment of enterprises in the vicinity of, and with the help of, universities is still another mechanism. We have all heard of the industrial parks in the United States and in Great Britain. Also, many other successful activities are being carried out, for instance, the incubator projects in the Netherlands and here in Sweden.

One must also consider general measures (*i.e.*, not directly oriented to regions or branches of industry), aimed at promoting technology transfer:

1. First, by increasing staff mobility — from the university to industry, *e.g.*, the sys-

tem of "researchers on loan" as practiced in Austria, the Technical Graduates for Industry Award System in Ireland, and the Danish Industrial Research Education Program—and also from industry to the university, *e.g.*, the Danish Cooperative Organization for Higher Education on Fyn and the German plans for postgraduate fellowships for practitioners;
2. Second, by the improved organization of technology transfer. Examples include:
   — Technological Information Centers;
   — the Liaison Offices in Great Britain; and
   — German Innovation Consultants' Agencies.

Other approaches for enhancing a particular capability in a selected branch of industry or new field include problem-oriented study courses and new study courses. Programs in microelectronics are an obvious case.

It is evident from the above examples that widely differing approaches are being tried out in order to strengthen the role of universities in contributing to economic development in any one country. This is more than mere groping for solutions and repeated attempts to master a difficult task. In this connection, we have not yet even discussed in depth what kind of economic development is actually desirable in the future.

In particular, the manifold approaches reflect the utterly different prerequisites in the individual countries. The extent to which research for economic development is conducted outside the universities is certainly important for the past and future roles played by these universities in this sector. In our countries the proportion of research carried out by industrial enterprises varies greatly. This is also true of the extent to which government-supported research institutions have been developed in addition to universities.

A Major Challenge

Such a condition certainly poses a major challenge to the universities. When something is to be done to enhance economic development, many countries place particular emphasis on the development of nonuniversity research. So far, much has been achieved on both sides. But, in view of tight budgets, stricter decisions will have to be made in this field. The difficult financial situation may also constitute a challenge to the universities to cooperate with industry more than in the past and to concentrate their efforts on projects which are important for economic development. The fact that this, in turn, may entail problems for the development of universities as a whole is not disputed.

Regional Approaches

First, we much reach agreement on what we understand by "regional." The United States and Canada, at any rate, themselves constitute extensive regions. In using the term "regional" here, I mean the cooperation in several countries within one particular geographic area.

I know of two examples, but am not sure whether they still apply:

— The first example was the University of East Africa in the 1960s. This institution's colleges were spread over Kenya, Tanzania, and Uganda. The Department of Veterinary Medicine in Nairobi was, for example, the sole facility in the entire region for training veterinary police officials. Perhaps its success was just a lucky incident between the period of colonialism and the gradual drifting apart of a group of states; at that time, however, it provided a convincing model precisely for developing countries.
— The second example is an association of the colleges and departments of forestry in Austria, Southern Germany, and the German-speaking area of Switzerland who joined forces after World War II to form a partnership of many years' duration. The common goal was the development of silvi-culture in Alpine countries.
— In addition, I should like to mention another example of the work of a university serving several countries in one particular region, namely, the American University in Beirut. This university worked towards the economic development of the countries of the Middle East beyond the borders of Lebanon. Because of political conditions, however, this work was limited and then stopped altogether.

The examples I have cited are, perhaps, somewhat exotic. A different statement is probably more appropriate to the countries from which we come: There may be isolated examples of university contributing to the development of a larger region, *i.e.,* an area extending across national borders, but this is the exception. Personally, I can see few approaches here even for the future in our highly-developed regions with a close network of universities and widely differing development problems.

I can see better opportunities for the developing countries, although probably two prerequisites are important in this case: first, sufficiently stable political conditions in the region in question, and second, gentle pressure from outside on the governments to stop staking out the limits of their sovereignity. The last point seems to me to be quite justified, however, provided that it is done in the right way, such as through the World Bank.

International Approaches and Tasks

After dealing with the national and regional aspects, let us now touch briefly on co-operation in the wider international context. This includes the participation of international organizations. The bigger the problems involved, the larger the size of the region in question and the larger the number of those participating, the more it becomes necessary to define and implement useful goals and concrete programs for universities, which might strengthen economic development. And yet there is surely something which can be done in this field. For example, the exchange of experience can be intensified, and recommendations can be made concerning national and regional initiatives. In this connection, international organizations, such as the OECD, have done good work, and can continue to do so in the future.

Major international programs are perhaps possible in individual cases, *e.g.,* geophysical programs concerning the utilization of the resources of the sea bed, the operation of earth observation satellites for the economic development of a region, or the improvement of the fishing industry in developing countries.

This brings me to my final consideration. The international aspect of the role of the universities in promoting economic development is not only a task for universities in the developing countries. On the contrary, there is also the task of developing the economy in the Third World. The contribution made by our universities in this respect can surely be increased further. Promising approaches in this connection are:

— partnerships established between universities in the developed and in the developing countries,
— cooperation of universities in development projects, and
— training of qualified staff from developing countries in the universities of the industrialized countries, to the extent that such training corresponds to the needs of the native countries of these experts.

Scandinavia provides the final example in this respect: the North Africa project started by Odense University in 1981.

Overview of Policy Issues: Panel Report on the Role of the Universities in Economic Development

Robert Chabbal

The questions passed by Valentin von Massow stimulated a discussion that paralleled the points he raised.

- Is it possible to ascertain the influence of universities on economic development?

The aggregate character and long-term orientation of universities make it very difficult to measure any concrete effects on the economy other than in some special cases, where several circumstances interact favorably. Silicon Valley (or perhaps "Siliclone" Valley is a more appropriate expression nowadays, considering the addition of biotechnology to the hitherto dominating electronics industry) is a recent example alongside the classical one of the establishment of the chemical industry on the basis of (then) new university research. The meaning of the term "economic development" may vary, however, and, with it, the evaluation of the universities. In high-technology countries, with high value-added industries, the role of universities is high-level, too, whereas in countries with "low-technology"/value-added branches of industry, the universities might well contribute to important improvements, but in less dramatic ways.

Also, the issue is closely related to what one means by the term "university" and its foremost aims, and whether one looks at old universities or newly-created ones. In the latter case, the act of establishing a new university or college in itself is often coupled to other political measures, not seldom of a regional development character. This may make it impossible to distinguish effects from causes, which decision-makers sometimes seem to forget.

Even though people's attitudes vary as to how actively universities should play their part, it is by now well recognized in most Western countries that they do participate in economic development. In Japan there is a view that this is not yet the general case there. Universities have traditionally been regarded as "consumers" only, spending state money, and not as "producers," contributing to the society's economic well-being. This has meant that the Japanese university system — despite its playing an instrumental role in the modernization of Japan after the Meiji restoration in the 1860s — has become rather isolated from other sectors of society, in-

Robert Chabbal is President of the Science and Technology Mission of the Ministry for Research and Industry, France.

cluding industry as well as state R&D units. Lately, suggestions have been put forward that the Science Council of Japan should undertake a study of the role of universities in economic development. Also professional economists are urged to include universities' role in their research on Japan's economic growth.

●   To what extent does the university aim to promote economic development?

On the one hand, the traditional "general" universities see education, training, and research as their main aims. Newer universities, along with many professional schools (*e.g.,* technical and agricultural universities), on the other hand, also are geared to promote industrial and economic development within their area of expertise or geographically. Or, as one could also put it, "since universities make big holes in the public purse, it is only fair that they should give something back."

Quite clearly, however, education and research are viewed as the fundamental role of universities for the traditional and newer universities, whatever additional goals they might have as well. Opinions differ though, as to the relative importance of "education" and "research."

Education Through Research

In France, for example, the *"grandes ecoles"* have had a direct impact on the French economy by their tradition of supplying well educated engineers, economists, etc. (*"les cadres"*). Here, *"formation par la recherche,"* education through research, is of utmost importance for the creation of good engineers and other professionals.

With universities, in contrast to professional schools, there is a risk: The best universities do excellent research in fields of high international interest. Thus these researchers want to teach their own specialties, which might be totally unrelated to the curricula of the university or to the needs of the region concerned. This could be the case not only in industrialized countries, but also in many Third World countries, where effects may well be adverse.

Research Facilities

Nevertheless, there is a need for universities and professional schools alike to have good research facilities both in order to recruit good faculty and, in particular, to pursue new technical areas. There are some interesting country differences to note.

In Finland, higher education authorities had chosen not to establish any new universities/colleges without research, which has been the case in Sweden. This has had some disadvantages, but in the United States there is a long tradition of four-year colleges without research; it is only in Europe that lack of research is an "innovation."

The fact that universities in a wide sense work mainly on a long-term basis makes it even more difficult to measure their contribution to the economic development of a country. In a time when even big industry pulls out of not only long-term, but also medium-term research, one view is that it is all the more important that universities stay where they are—sometimes even to the "left of basic research" (on a time axis) as a counter-balancing factor. Thus in Japan, for example, industry warns universities not to become too short-term oriented.

The supplying of professional talent is considered one of a university's most important contributions to industrial and hence economic development. Here traditions vary between countries, depending on several factors. For example, Swedish industry historically has not been inclined to demand a post-graduate degree in its recruitment of R&D personnel, whereas abroad, it is a very common practice, as in Germany, and often a formal requirement.

In some fast-moving, priority research areas, industry in a few countries like the United States cannot wait for universities to produce enough masters and doctors. Companies hire frequently at completion of the baccalaureate process, not without risk for the continued development in the fields in question, since this in a way amounts to "eating the seed corn."

The Innovation Cycle

One last point deserves attention when surveying the extent to which the university promotes economic development, and that relates to the role university research may play in the innovation cycle. While it is not the objective of academia to focus solely on research that has direct commercial application, there are instances—notably in microelectronics—where "market pull" can continue with the research and educational resources of a university to yield, through a development process, a new product or process. The role of the university in these cases touches upon new business development and the commercialization of university research.

There has been concern that this type of activity will create pressures that could divert traditional university goals. Most of the concern rests with the obligations of faculty members, rather than on indirect effects on university activities. Different universities have designed institutional arrangements to accommodate this type of research, and these arrangements—through a variety of approaches—generally address such issues as faculty time, extent of industrial support, and royalties from patents and licensing. In the United States, there are several examples, including Stanford Center for Integrated Systems; Robotics Institute, Carnegie-Mellon University; Cornell Industry Research Park; Engenics; and Hoechst AT—Massachusetts General (a Harvard affiliate).

● Does one have to take new measures in order to develop the role of universities in economic development?

Policies for governing ties between universities and other sectors of society vary widely. In Germany, for instance, the universities are supposed to fulfill primarily the role of education. Research is the private responsibility of the individual professors and scientists. Contacts with industry, contract research, and so forth are thus conducted on a private basis. Consequently, it is in this German case somewhat inaccurate to speak of university—industry relations in a "collective" sense, which, on the other hand, is often the case in the United States. Perhaps it could be said that most European countries, when it comes to regulation of inter-action, fall somewhere in between these two examples.

It is often claimed that universities are badly equipped to serve small- and medium-sized enterprises, and that they concentrate too heavily on relating to big industry. One has to distinguish between research-intensive small companies and other enterprises, however, as well as between new and traditional areas of activity within large companies. Further, there are university fields with little or no contact with the world outside academia. Depending on the case, different paths must be pursued in order to change attitudes on the university side as well as on the part of companies and other potential users of academic work and research results. Here, too, the communication between individuals is vital for any mechanism to be established.

● Approaches towards achieving improvements within the national framework.

The question of facilitating mechanisms for interaction on a national level relates to the role of universities in a country's policy for regional development. There are examples of universities being established in areas that are geographically distant or traditionally rural: in Sweden around Lulea in the far north, and in the northern Jutland area of Denmark. An interesting case is the siting of a new Dutch univers-ity in the southern part of the country with a faculty mix of medicine, economics, and a school for interpreters, which has had minimal impact on the surrounding area. In contrast, a new university has been established in northern Finland, along with a state research center and several industries, which has had a more substantial impact.

There are several types of mechanisms common to different countries which serve to enhance university interactions:

- Local extension and information services at universities: Ireland, Denmark, Finland, Germany.
- Programs to assist entrepreneurs/new ventures: France, Ireland, the UK, the US, Finland.
- Science/industrial parks: US, South France, UK, Finland, Holland. One notes that these "parks" seldom seem to aid small- to medium-size enterprises, but rather appeal to big companies.
- Exchange of personnel
  a. "adjunct professors" (industrialists as part-time university teachers, *e.g.*, in the Netherlands, Sweden);
  b. "researchers on loan" (university staff to industry, *e.g.*, in Austria, Ireland, Sweden); and
  c. liaison offices at universities (Germany, US, UK, and others).

In addition to contract research, universities may carry out "contract education" as well, and tailor a certain curriculum or individual courses for a given technical group as defined by a customer company. Some big international high-technology companies have such advanced in-house programs, however, that they are equal or superior to their best national universities in qualified manpower as well as equipment. Examples here could be found in Germany as well as the UK.

Collaborative Efforts

There are a few international collaborative efforts in education which are worth noting. There is a joint program involving Japan and South East Asia whereby nationals of South East Asia can acquire a doctorate through a Japanese university. Most of the work is completed in the national's home institution in coordination with the participating Japanese university. Only about 12 months of study in the program is required in Japan. The Asian Institute of Technology (AIT) in Bangkok serves as another illustration. This is supported by various state agencies as well as private foundations in Asia, as well as the US and Europe. It includes temporary employment of outstanding professors from the contributing countries. The school produces a considerable proportion of the next generation of decision–makers in government and industry in Asia's market economies.

Universities have a very important means of contributing to the long-term economic development of their countries through accepting foreign students and researchers, who will eventually promote trade in goods and know-how with their former host country. Although a tightening economic situation may mean that special fees have to be charged, the British experience serves as a reminder: The number of visiting students, mainly from the Commonwealth, declined drastically when fees were increased, thus totally offsetting the intended effect.

To facilitate international cooperation between universities and industry, NATO has launched a new program to improve mobility in the civil, applied R&D sector. Drawing on the success of their programs for collaboration between basic researchers in different countries — including non-member ones — they have now introduced a similar scheme intended for academic as well as industrial scientists.

University Participation in Strategic Business Planning

William R. Dill

I have three problems with my assigned topic. First of all, strategic planning is not something that every firm does. In fact, very few corporations really do it—and even fewer do it well. Few colleges and universities even attempt it, and most of us who have tried it have little to show in the way of results.

The scope of the task is immense. Strategic planners are expected to accomplish more than wizards in the courts of ancient kings. They are expected to pull clear concepts of trends, opportunities, and limits from messy data about messy environments. They are asked to frame statements of mission and suggestions for goals that will affect decisions long beyond the time horizon for which they can make confident predictions. They are agents for change, but—at the same time— prisoners of what a company is and has been.

Second, although a planning effort draws on experts of many kinds, the heart of the effort involves coming to terms with people in the firm who have responsibility for action. A planning document means little unless it relates to the lives and work of the people who must carry it out.

Third, planning presumes some power to predict and to make sense out of the disorder in complex environments. Too many efforts at strategic planning have become "muscle bound" in their assumptions about the tractibility of the world that a firm confronts. The reality—to which strategic planning approaches are still being adapted—is that we must plan in the face of great uncertainty and ignorance about even the near-term future.

How Universities Might Help

Nevertheless, with faith that serious efforts at strategic planning have some value, let us look at the question of how universities might help. We will focus on three possible ways:

- *Shared efforts.* As colleges and universities themselves begin to plan, there are many ways in which they can usefully join forces with corporate planning

William R. Dill is President of Babson College in Massachusetts.

groups, at least in common analysis of the environment with which both must deal.

- *Diversifying and enriching sources of information and advice.* Universities, by their nature, house few people who might run a corporation, but many who are experts in fields from which corporate planners can draw as they do their work.

- *"Stirring the pot" to make sure the corporation moves when planning fails.* Many of the most profound changes in large corporations come, not as the result of strategic planning, but from the "kick in the pants" of new entrepreneurial competition. Universities in some parts of the world have an excellent record of helping to launch new businesses that demand a response from larger, established enterprises.

Joint Efforts in Planning

Although universities are anything but "unitary," goal-driven organizations, and although most have been rather loosely managed, events are forcing them to learn how to plan. Large private and multi-campus state systems in the United States face difficult problems of changing audiences and of limited resources, especially in a decade when the annual influx of college-age students will be shrinking by 25% to 35%. New competition from industrial education programs and new technologies for education, such as telecommunications and the computer, have changed possibilities and priorities for us. Even some smaller colleges like Babson have developed strategic plans to sort out their future emphases in education and research.

Already in the United States universities and companies collaborate in planning by exchanging personnel. A college like Babson or a university like Carnegie-Mellon or MIT takes advantage of the business leaders who serve on its board of trustees. They are not figureheads, but active partners in deciding how the school should evolve. We also draw in many other people from industry as members of visiting committees for projects and departments, or as adjunct faculty. In return, many of us serve on corporate boards of directors or in active roles as consultants and advisers to industry. Even some of Babson's graduate students work with companies, as part of their education, on major planning projects.

What is new, though, is the development in the United States of a variety of joint business-university task forces to work on major joint planning assignments. In Massachusetts, for example, there is a High Technology Council, which has worked to improve the development climate for electronic and biogenetic firms, and to assure adequate flows of well trained technical talent and relevant research from the universities. On a joint European-American basis, companies and schools recently finished a two-year exploration of the likely demands that will be placed on managers in the early years of the next century. American companies and universities have worked together to determine how both can adapt better to the growing predominance of international trade and markets.

If there is a limit to these efforts, it has two aspects. Too often the joint consultations involve people who are not central to the planning effort within either the firm or the university. Too often, as well, the collaboration takes a "one shot" form, like this conference — rather than a multi-year commitment to development and follow-up.

The opportunities for collaboration are great, but they require participation by key people and support and cultivation over time. Among the specific fields for collaboration worth examining are these:

- In relation to technology, joint exploration of how opportunities and needs in the marketplace fit to the development of new scientific and technological possibilities.
- In relation to our common problem of building a stronger human resource base for industry and society, joint exploration of how we handle the task of lifelong education and re-education.
- In the political and cultural arena, joint studies of the interdependence between technology and economics on the one side with political and social realities on the other.

Providing Talent from the University

The second major way that universities can contribute to corporate planning — by making new kinds of talent and expertise available — is perhaps closest to the theme of this conference. Experts, however, are a mixed blessing. Look at what two highly "degreed" scientists thought about aviation in 1910:

- "It is idle to look for a commercial future for the flying machine. . . . There are some . . . who will argue that because a machine will carry two people, another may be constructed that will carry a dozen. But those who make this contention do not understand the theory of weight sustention in the air; or that the greater the load the greater must be the lifting power . . . and that there is a limit to these . . . beyond which the aviator cannot go."

In 1958 we misjudged the market for computers as badly, and in 1974 we began planning for a long-term energy crisis in which many argued that oil prices would never decline again. Louis Robinson of IBM observed recently that, if you think you know where technology is going, the only sure thing is that you will be disappointed. We know that change will occur, but it "is in the ignorance of what that change is that we will have to work."

With those reservations about experts, how can companies make better use of the expertise that universities have to offer, not just in engineering and science, but in economics, politics, world cultures, human behavior, law, and other fields relevant to strategic planning? The answer lies in four steps: strategic sensitivity, proximity, structure and continuity, and incentives.

- *Strategic sensitivity.* You will get better strategic advice from experts, if they are trained to understand the nature of strategic problems. Universities have begun to build the concepts of strategic analysis solidly into their management programs, but the same emphasis ought to be more a part of the education of engineers and scientists. The traditional course in engineering economics focuses on equipment replacement, rather than on broader understanding of how markets and economic factors shape the allocation of resources for the development and use of technology. If there is not room for such a course in the early part of engineering and science education, it certainly is a good topic for a mid-career program. Babson is offering such courses, in fact, not only to engineers, but to people working in other fields, such as human resource management.

Strategic sensitivity is also enhanced by encouraging radical forms of job rotation. Professors need more than consulting experience and occasional visits by people from industry to the campus to understand industry's needs. It ought to be far more common than it is for a professor to take a two-to-five-year leave of absence from the university to work on assignments in business where strategic questions will be faced and dealt with, and for academic departments to absorb similar medium-term visitors from industry to become integral members of their teaching and research activities for a while.

- *Proximity.* Perhaps the only valid proposition in social psychology is that people who spend time in proximity to one another tend to interact with one another. Proximity is such a simple idea that we tend to overlook it, but when one analyzes the success of business-university interactions around Boston, in California's Silicon Valley, or in the Research Triangle of North Carolina, proximity is an important stimulus for the synergy that has developed.

- *Structure and Continuity.* It is relatively easy to solve the problem of getting access to an individual expert on a sustained basis, but universities and corporations need to do more to assure sustained collaborative efforts between groups. The Wharton Econometric Model effort and the PIMMS Marketing Strategy Resource Center at Harvard are two examples of very successful build-up of university-based groups to help companies plan, but each took extraordinarily dedicated leadership, innovative concessions from the university, and lots of corporate funding to develop.

We at Babson have not set up group structures for research, but we have put together a multi-company consortium for executive education. Keeping it going requires a commitment of long-term faculty participation from us and an equally long-sighted agreement to participation by the top management of the six companies involved.

Once something is well established, it is sometimes possible to expand its base of operations. An interesting development with the Wharton Model, for example, is that this now has pieces being prepared by several universities around the world, thus providing a strong international base that adds to its value for corporate planners.

- *Incentives.* Corporations which want universities to help them with strategic planning must reckon with the need to provide incentives for the experts whom they want to give them sustained and dedicated service. This problem varies with the country — contrast, for example, the rules in Japan against professors accepting compensation for consulting with the very entrepreneurial search by American professors for outside income. Corporations seeking university help, though, must recognize that professors and the universities themselves have several other priorities that generally come ahead of helping Company X develop a strategic plan. Whether the rewards go to the individual professors, to the department, or to the institution as a whole, corporations do have to make it attractive for the experts to shift their priorities.

"Stirring the Pot" — Universities and Entrepreneurship

For all we may talk about planning, the fact remains that the biggest contribution that universities can make to large corporations is to throw sand in their faces by helping to launch new enterprises. Large companies — even ones with good planning systems — tend to be clumsy about early development of really new products and markets. It was Apple Computer, as much as internal foresight, that shaped IBM's entry into the personal computer market. Upstarts like Xerox and Savin-Ricoh built a photocopying industry from scratch. Entrepreneurs named Honda and Toyota forced General Motors and British Leyland to develop an entirely new approach to strategy for the 1980s.

The contribution of colleges and universities to the entrepreneurial process is dear to my heart as President of Babson, because — as a small college — we have historically been identified more with starting new businesses than with supplying functionaries to the world's largest industrial bureaucracies. Big companies always plan with too much memory of what they have been in the past, and too often with assumptions of immortality which the canons of free enterprise never intended.

After years of almost total neglect, when only a few schools like Babson gave the subject any attention, many universities are now emphasizing entrepreneurship in both their management and their engineering programs. These include courses for young men and women, as well as for more experienced people, who may be right on the verge of launching a business.

But the effort goes beyond courses and research. Several schools, such as MIT, Rensselaer and Stanford, have developed reputations as "incubators" for small businesses started around ideas coming from their laboratories. Others, like Babson, without technical laboratories as part of their resources, are still encouraging the "incubation" of small businesses as a way of giving students an early start toward having enterprises of their own. Control Data is an example of a large corporation which has made a major commitment to encouraging entrepreneurship through data services, training programs, advisory assistance, and a network of business and technology centers in which new small firms can find a home for their early developments.

Incubation can have spectacular results. Control Data claims that only 14% of the firms — as opposed to the usual expectation of 70%–80% — in their first business and technology center have folded after the first three years of operation.

Our skills in spotting and training entrepreneurs and in assisting the growth of new firms are still being developed, but we see this as a major area for university experimentation in the next decade.

Some Final Questions

Looking ahead, there is obviously a great deal still to be done to encourage and channel university participation in strategic planning and strategic encouragement of entrepreneurial competition for business. My agenda for helping to speed up that process includes trying to find answers to these questions:

- How can companies and universities work together better to develop agendas and structures for cooperative analysis of the environment — the problems and opportunities, the uncertainties and risks — that both must cope with?
- How do we help both line managers in companies and experts with useful talents in the university to develop a better sense of strategic analysis and its role in plotting futures for both universities and industry?
- How do we create innovative structures and incentives to encourage more sustained working relationships between experts in the universities and business, in ways that respect their separate roles in society and the detachment that each must maintain from the other?
- How do we encourage more of a spirit of entrepreneurship, both to provide competitive challenges to large organizations and to provide internal support for innovation and change within these organizations?
- How can we bring schools of technology and schools of management within the university together to work on common elements of these tasks?

This last question deserves some comment, because — in my experience — we are talking about problems where both engineering and management faculties ought to be working together. Even in schools like MIT and Carnegie-Mellon, however, where both such faculties exist, the interactions are weak. If we in the universities are to challenge businesses to seek new relationships with us, we must be prepared to work from within to break down traditional school and departmental barriers that make little sense when confronted with the broad dimensions of strategic problems.

Overview of Policy Issues:
Panel Report on University Participation
in Strategic Business Planning

Pierre Aigrain and Gunnar Blockmar

Before addressing the topic of interaction between universities and industry in strategic planning and long-range business planning, one must first cover the more general problems of the role of strategic planning in business today. As William Dill pointed out ". . . strategic planning is not something that every firm does. In fact, very few corporations really do it—and even fewer do it well. Few colleges and universities even attempt it, and most of us who have tried have little to show in the way of results."

This reflects the present situation very well. Using strategic planning and long-range planning has been more popular in the past than it is at the present time. The general tendency in a rapidly changing environment is more to gear the company for flexibility than to try to predict the future.

It is necessary to make a distinction here between long-range planning and strategic business planning. Long-range planning can be regarded as decisions based on forecasts. A number of business indicators are selected and studied for a number of time periods. Based on these time series, one then tries to predict the future development of these indicators. Decisions are based on these forecasts to adapt the business to the predicted future.

Strategic planning implies decisions in different matters. When product life cycles are getting shorter, the key issue is to plan for flexibility. The strategic plan sets a target to work for and the decisions aim at fulfilling this plan, taking into account the rapid changes that may be necessary.

Having made this distinction, one still finds that more of forecasting and less of strategic planning has been the common practice in many firms. This leads to a very important question: How does one make a company react fast enough to *technical* changes? Can the universities aid in solving this problem?

Back to the Ivory Towers?

There is a concern that the very extrovert orientation of universities now is only a fading wave. The hard economic situation for universities in many countries makes

Pierre Aigrain is Scientific Adviser to the president of Thomson, and is the former Secretary of State for Science and Technology, France.

Gunnar Blockmar is affiliated with the Royal Swedish Academy of Engineering Sciences.

them more inclined to take on research financed by industry. As soon as the hard times have passed, researchers may return to their "ivory towers," where they have dwelt before, as in the late 1960s and early 1970s.

This view is, however, not justified by the development of relationships. There are several long-term contracts for research relationships between industry and universities. One example is the relationship between Westinghouse and Carnegie-Mellon; another is Center for Integrated Systems at Stanford University. In the new and rapidly expanding biotechnology field, many leading professors are in one way or another connected to an industrial company. And, in fact, one role of universities can be to conserve and develop knowledge and competence when industry is not capable of promoting the long term development sufficiently fast on its own, or when the marketable result is too far away to be interesting for financiers.

Motives for Cooperation

According to Dr. Dill of Babson College, the motives for cooperation between industry and university can be characterized by three keywords:

- Partnership
- Expertise
- Provocation

Partnership is already taking many shapes as shared activities, with cross memberships on boards, advisory and consulting groups, and student projects. It might however be that this form of cooperation is more developed in the United States than in other countries. Many obstacles exist, both legal and "cultural," and will take considerable effort to eliminate.

The possibility of partnership and interaction between different faculties of a university must also be considered. Creating links between schools of technology and schools of business management should be given high priority.

Expertise in itself is not necessarily a good guide for long-range and strategic planning. Bad examples abound. But today industry needs to know not only what to choose, but *how* to choose. Knowing to which criteria the selection of technology must be made is of great importance, and is possibly an area for cooperation in the future.

The common assumption is that the area of technology with the best opportunity for cooperation is the main line of business of a company. For example, an electronics company should be best served by close contact with departments of electronics at a university. However, this might not be the case. A company has its own very advanced competence in this subject. The equipment is usually very modern, often more modern than a university can afford. Moreover, industry researchers have more resources and funds for their work.

The best opportunity for collaboration may well be in a totally different area, say, chemistry. Here, the competence of an electronics company may be more limited. The addition of competence in chemistry from a university offers greater opportunities for new, interesting and promising combinations of the two disciplines.

The "provoking" role of the university is twofold. The first is in identifying and analyzing new trends in technology. By making industry aware of a developing technology early, industry may react on a more timely basis.

The second role is to promote the use of technological information in the overall strategic planning process. A large company sometimes does not rely very much on technological input in its strategic planning process. The university could act to increase the awareness of this information.

Summing Up

For an industrial company, technical competence is only one factor affecting strategic business planning. To increase the importance of this factor is also to increase the importance of strategic planning in general for a company. Universities can aid in this development by supplying knowledge in many ways, through the transfer of graduates, through research faculty. A variety of mechanisms with informal contacts between universities and industry are essential.

Compatibility of University Integrity with Industrial Cooperation

Jürgen Starnick and Jürgen Allesch

Stagnating economic growth and an increasing number of unemployed form the framework that, in many industrial countries, raises the question of "technical progress" and "innovation" to a central starting point for many activities in economic policies. Thus also the universities have become a focus of public interest.

Today it is not the sole task of a university—and especially of a technical university—to guarantee the education of a sufficient number of highly qualified junior laborers and to be engaged in the research of new technical knowledge. Rather, it has become a central task of the universities, to a larger extent, to make accessible to industry the results of their research and development activities.

Before I point out more precisely these aspects through the example of the Technical University of Berlin, permit me a short historical retrospective with regard to the development of technical universities in Germany and their functions for the economy and society. A recourse for history may also be permitted, because this easily leads to the question of which role falls to the scientific field—mainly, however, to the Technical University of Berlin for which I speak—with regard to today's development and improvement of relations between universities and enterprises.

The development of Germany in becoming a leading industrial nation is again and again pointed to as a "unique road" through European history. In many cases these opinions revolve around the concept of "delay" or the so-called "delayed nation," "delayed industrialization," or "delayed modernization of business and industry." These terms are, not without reason, a firm component of many historical views with regard to Germany's economic history. They point to the long and often stony road of German industrialization since the beginning of the 19th century. Among German countries, the state of Prussia with its capital, Berlin, played a major role in the numerous efforts to cope with the respective "delays."

Two phases of the industrialization of Germany are particularly significant with regard to national efforts to further research, development, and educational institutions. The first phase, which can be dated at about the end of the 18th cen-

Jürgen Starnick is President of the Technical University of Berlin, where he is a Professor of Chemical Engineering.

Jürgen Allesch is Director of the Technology Transfer Office of the Technical University of Berlin.

tury, was characterized by the endeavors of Prussia, the largest German state at that time — disregarding Austria for the time being — to make up for its fundamental backwardness in industrial development as compared with France and England. The establishment of a vocational institute served as the most important instrument for the national promotion of economic interests; this institute was one of the predecessors of today's Technical University in Berlin. According to modern terminology, this vocational institute became the earliest technology transfer agency.

Besides stimulating a vocational education for future enterprise that was primarily practice-oriented, a main task of the institute consisted of the reproduction and further development of machinery from France and England. The principles of this machinery were transmitted to the manufacturer with the help of exhibitions. Until about the middle of the century, the official policy was to educate technical intelligentsia and support technological mediation. This had the result that Prussia was again brought into connection with general industrial development.

The Second Phase

The second phase of the industrialization process occurred toward the end of the 19th century and approximately converges with the date of the founding of the Technical University of Berlin. In 1879, this university arose as the Royal Technical School of Higher Education in Berlin from the incorporation of the vocational academy with the older building academy. This was the same year in which the first electrically driven train from Werner Siemens was presented at the Vocational Exhibition in Berlin. And this was the time that the development of high voltage technology had introduced a revolution in production techniques.

The year 1879 marks concurrently the historical commencement of an intensive escalation in national promotion for scientific systems, especially through the construction of technical schools of higher education. Immediately after this followed the establishment of one of the first academic chairs for electrical technology and, from 1904 on, Georg Schlesinger taught in the new subject area, "Machine Tools and Factory Management." After World War I, this same Schlesinger publicly worked for the mechanization of German industry along the lines formulated by Winslow Taylor.

In history, monocausal explanations of any and every type are bound to fail. This is true as well for explaining the relationship between science and educational systems on the one hand, and industrial and social innovation on the other. Nevertheless, we may ascertain that the situation of a "delay" existed; that is, of a situation in which technological innovations — and, thereby, also the economic innovations which are based upon technology — were retarded relative to the possibilities of the time. This situation necessitated carefully planned national action. The economic renewal, which did not develop naturally of itself, had to be achieved with the guiding help of the state. The state reacted to this task by constructing an educational and scientific system, and twice it proved successful.

In the first phase, which one could call the "take-off" phase, it was successful in comparison to the completely comparable situation in today's developing countries. And then again, it was successful in the second phase, which is concerned with concentrating upon placing the now-ready, highly developed technological knowledge and a highly-developed industrial structure at the front lines of world-wide technological and industrial progress.

I hope that this rather comprehensive retrospect over the historical development of technical universities in Germany has provided, in rough outline, an impression of the historical basis for today's work at technical universities. However, before I come to speak about today's situation at technical universities in Germany, let me add a remark which I find essential to our topic.

This recourse to history has hopefully helped to elucidate that the development of universities oriented toward the natural sciences and technology was in all phases closely related to current and foreseen industrial requirements. This has always been and still is the case today. It is important not only for mere principles of self-preservation; it is the decisive presupposition for scientific work. Which role do technical universities play today, and how do we understand technology transfer at the Technical University of Berlin?

Complex Conditions

At this point, it can be said without exaggeration that conditions in today's universities are by far more complex regarding scientific work, as well as technology transfer, compared to earlier phases. We need only think of the complexity of scientific processes, which lie hidden behind a term like "teamwork" or "interdisciplinary research." But also in the very specialized structures of highly modern industries, a totally new situation for universities has originated.

I am thinking of the "discovery" of the innovative potential of small- and medium-sized companies that, due to the well-known Schumpeter thesis—that only large enterprises are capable of innovation—had been neglected by the state with partly serious consequences. But, moreover, a technical university today has the task in the area of research not only to offer new lumps of scientific and technological understanding to industry, but, more than that, has taken over the duty of actively taking an interest itself in the introduction and successful transplantation of technical advances to the enterprise. In doing this, the opening up of the university to industrial interests, above all, should not—and must not—lead to an "industrialization" of higher education. Without doubt there is a great challenge to the university here—but also a change.

A modern technical university can no longer withdraw into the often-attested "ivory tower"—if this metaphor may be permitted here—but it must actively take part in the often difficult and protracted process of preparing both enterprises and science for the practically oriented employment of new technology. In the last few years, a positive process of rethinking has undoubtedly been set in motion, not only on the one hand in what concerns the sensibilities of many—above all, the younger scientists for the requirements of the economy—but also in what concerns the enterprises' conviction for the warranted interests of science on the other hand. Because of this, then, in my opinion, we find ourselves at the beginning of a process which will continue a long while, but, notwithstanding that, is a necessary process.

For this reason, the Technical University of Berlin, in my opinion, is an example for other universities in the Federal Republic of Germany. In recognition of new tasks of science in cooperation with current national departments, a number of arrangements has been developed, which I would like to discuss. Allow me, please, to make a fundamental comment here at the beginning which, above all, stands at the forefront of our considerations. The successful transfer of new scientific understanding from research fields to their use in industry depends to a great degree upon personal initiative, and the creation of a consolidated and mutual confidence of all participating persons in the transfer and innovation process. Accordingly, the availability of financial resources can only have a supportive function here. Our experience to date also points out that these factors are of a special significance precisely for technology transfer in small- and medium-sized enterprises.

Technology Transfer in Practice

Now then, how does technology transfer at the Technical University of Berlin actually take place in practice? In order to intensify the technology transfer between the Berlin economy and the research institutions and universities in Berlin, in 1980 the Technical University Transfer program (TU Transfer) was founded as a central information point of request from the economy. Since then more than 400 inquiries have been dealt with, and cooperation contacts with scientific institutions have been mediated. Technology mediation, as understood by the Technical University, comprises five essential transfer sections:

- Information Transfer
  The knowledge of the latest state of technology worldwide provides a base for management decisions oriented to the future, and thus may assist in preventing bad investments. According to on-line-concept and with the help of data processing, the present state of any technology can be ascertained at more than 250 publications data banks and for almost all scientific fields. This collected knowledge can be used to effect the goals of research and development plans for business.
- Technology Transfer
  When inquiries from enterprises come in, the TU Transfer mediates and supports the transaction of cooperative projects with scientists and institutes of the universities and other public research establishments in Berlin (this is termed "research referred inquiry development").

  For scientific development based upon economically oriented developments, the TU Transfer supports scientists in their search for business partners with whom they may cooperate so that their own developments may be economically utilized. On the occasion of the fair at Hannover in 1983, a "Berlin research market" will be introduced as a special attraction. This market will show more than 400 products, procedures and services as cooperation offerings of Berlin research institutions to the Berlin economy.

- Technologically Oriented Enterprise Foundations
  The foundation of enterprises based on technology represents an important branch of scientific transfer mediated by the university. The readiness of scientists to become economically independent has steadily increased. TU Transfer supports the readiness of young creative scientists to utilize their knowledge in an independent existence by motivating them and giving them assistance through information seminars, management advice, and providing the use of laboratories and workshop facilities at the universities.
- Personnel Transfer
  Enterprises can only recognize technological developments in their own fields and make use of them if they have qualified personnel at their disposal. The presence of qualified junior personnel in development and management as mediators of modern "know-how" will in the long run be the most effective form of technology transfer. The entry of graduates into small- and medium-sized enterprises as mediators of "know-how" will be eased through such a personnel transfer program.
- Regional Qualification Programs
  In cooperation with other public and private institutions of further education, re-education and qualifications programs will be developed and carried out for regional problem areas. In preparation are qualification programs in artificial materials technology and microelectronics.

All these fields, working together to complement and mutually support one another, must be considered as the precondition for the transfer of scientific information. The technical universities, then, must accept the function of a "pathfinder," since presumably only they are in the position to bear such a conception. We, however, stand now at only the beginning of such a development. The prerequisite, especially for the institutes of higher education—and I stress this explicitly once again—is the cautious but steady construction of cooperative relations between research and industrial practice in accordance with the complete standards of scientific autonomy at the technical universities. Seen this way, the Technical University of Berlin understands the transfer of scientific information not only as a debt paid to all business fields outside the university, but also as an opportunity for the university itself.

Overview of Policy Issues:
Panel Report on Compatibility of University Integrity with Industrial Cooperation

Hugo Thiemann

Any discussion of university integrity and the ways in which it might be threatened by intensified university-industry research interactions must be based on some conception of the societal role of the university. Herein lies a major difficulty, for there are many signs that the role of the research university is currently undergoing rapid change.

The general economic stagnation we are experiencing is forcing this change in two ways. First, government funding is perceived as a less secure source of support for university research than before, with most governments under strong pressure to reduce budget deficits. Second, there is an assumption that the universities represent an unexploited resource that could usefully contribute to reviving the economy. On a general level, this assumption appears to be shared by all three parties involved, *i.e.,* government, industry and the universities themselves. On a more concrete level, the expectation may, however, vary considerably between the parties involved.

Traditionally, university research has been viewed predominantly as an adjunct to the university's teaching function. During the period in which universities were rapidly growing, this bias was further emphasized by the fact that university teaching provided ample work opportunities for research scientists. This also explains why universities during this period, in many respects, became more introverted and self-contained with weakened external contacts. However, with stagnating, and in some cases declining, student enrollment, the "teaching market" has become saturated, motivating universities to find an external market for their research staff. As a consequence, the actual content of university research and its relevance to nonacademic pursuits are acquiring increasing significance.

Crucial questions in the present context are, then: In what sense, how far, and through which mechanisms should university research capabilities be matched with problems of particular industrial significance?

Hugo Thiemann is a member of the Board of the Swiss Academy of Engineering Sciences.

The University Role and Industry

Types of Research

Universities are in a unique position to carry out exploratory and broadly based research, which should remain the core of the university research program. The more narrowly focused research, which universities pursue through contracts, should thus supplement the variety of university research without unduly influencing the basic program. This premise is consistent with the interest of most companies who collaborate with universities. The primary motivation rests in gaining access to a fundamental understanding of certain phenomena of importance to some aspect of a company's activities.

Though less pronounced, other types of research are also of interest to industry. Small companies, for example, may emphasize the need for help on practical short-term problems. Programs reflecting the common interests of several companies, usually conducted on a multi-year basis, is another type of research which industry pursues in collaboration with universities.

Impact of Funding

Funding can be a major mechanism affecting the pattern of research at a university. For example, government will most likely continue to provide the dominant source of funding for university research. Grants and contracts could be distributed, at least partly, on the basis of industrial support that different groups have been able to attract. In this case, government funds could either reinforce a research area with supplemental funds, or contribute to a balanced mix of research by funding areas not receiving industry support.

A significant responsibility for universities is the distribution of discretionary resources. Spread too thinly over too many research programs, areas of potential research excellence may be diluted. The threshold costs for maintaining a viable research effort have increased dramatically and the choice of research areas to be pursued actively is becoming a strategic question of great importance to every university. Actual or potential industrial interests are thus important factors to be considered in a coherent decision-making process. This includes the development of key programs which avoids an over-reliance on any individual source of funding.

Products

The utility and desirability of matching university research with industrial needs will vary a great deal between research areas, industries, and countries. Some large companies have considerable research resources of their own. It is, however, becoming increasingly difficult, even for the larger companies, to maintain quality research in all areas important to the company and, consequently, the need to work closely with external research groups should be increasing.

In some countries and some research areas there are other research institutions besides universities with whom industry can cooperate. The ability of the universities to maintain or strengthen their research position in relation to other noncorporate research establishments will depend on a number of factors, many of which are specific to each country. The outcome will, of course, have a bearing on where industry will look for research partnerships. There is, however, likely to be a bias on the part of industry in favor of universities, since they have two "products" to offer, namely, trained people and research capabilities. Industry's demand for a research product is often difficult to distinguish from its interest in finding trained people. In fact, some of the industrial support to university research has training as its main objective to secure industry's need for qualified manpower. Nonetheless, the importance to industry of the universities' research appears to be growing, depending on the depth of its own R&D efforts.

Administrative Structure

As the societal relevance of university research receives greater emphasis, it is only natural that many universities discover that their existing administrative structures need to be overhauled or supplemented to facilitate research interactions with industry. Much needs to be done in most universities to make information about ongoing research more accessible to groups outside the university.

Real-world problems are interdisciplinary in nature, and industry often seeks a competence integrating diverse approaches and different disciplines. The university, however, in its present structure, enhances the formation of disciplinary specialists. Universities may introduce new administrative structures or organizations to bridge this gap and to facilitate a dialogue. In some instances, special research centers, which usually operate successfully, have been set up on or near a university campus, administratively separated from the university, to do contract research.

Commercial Applications of University Research

While technical development work is outside the mainline business of the university, with the exception of engineering schools, considerable attention is presently being given to alternative ways of helping to commercialize ideas of new products or processes that have sprung out of university research. The question has arisen as to whether the university should engage itself in the launching and nurturing of such new ventures. Notwithstanding the fact that several path-breaking innovations can be traced back to university research, the record of past attempts to systematically help commercialize innovative ideas emanating from its research is not totally encouraging. Marketing is often a major stumbling block, requiring much larger resources than the scientists expect. In other words, the present high expectations on universities' ability to derive income from commercial ventures appear likely to be disappointed.

Serious conflicts of interest can arise when individual faculty members launch their own companies to exploit their academic research. Often the faculty members concerned will have to make a choice, in such situations, between an academic career and a business career.

Universities as a rule seem more willing to accept, and in some cases actively encourage, their faculty members to consult with companies on a limited scale. Although there are occasional cases of abuse in consulting relationships, most universities have experienced arrangements that are successful and appropriate. It is clearly to the benefit of the university that their faculty members are aware of the latest technical developments in industry, and consulting work has proved to be a useful mechanism for achieving this. In areas where industrial technology is developing rapidly, there may, however, be a need to go further than a consulting relationship, and an exchange of personnel between universities and industry may be arranged. Universities will benefit from keeping many parallel channels of communication to industry open, particularly through personal contacts.

University Integrity

Maintaining university integrity cannot be interpreted to mean a closing off of communication between universities and industry. Universities need close contacts with industry for a dialogue between research on campus and its application and utility in society. This process, in turn, yields new challenges for university research. To retain and improve its integrity, universities should actively develop contacts with many "stakeholders," thereby increasing their independence, enhancing their channels of information, and ensuring a plurality of interests. This implies a greater effort on the part of universities to understand the problems of industry, and to define and communicate their strengths to potential stakeholders. It also implies that universities have an obligation to define their own strategies for establishing ongoing areas of research excellence.

Summing Up

Ingvar Carlsson

A number of the national economies of the Western world — as of the world at large — are currently facing very serious problems. The strength and vitality of the enterprise sectors will, therefore, be decisive for future development. For the active industrial policy that the present situation demands, technological innovation and high-quality R&D efforts will be of crucial importance.

Against that background, the issues that have been raised during these discussions and the prospects that have been presented are not only central for industrial planning, but are also at the heart of political interest. The fact that this conference is organized as a cooperative initiative by the Swedish Employment Security Council and the New York University Center for Science and Technology Policy is in itself significant of the present situation. It is also encouraging as an indication of a trend towards greater understanding of the interrelationship of the different actors on the scene.

The interdependence between industry and research establishments has been further highlighted through the themes selected for this conference. My concluding remarks will present the view of a politician. It is now more imperative than ever that everyone join in working for the continuing development of industrialized society — economically, as well as socially and culturally.

More than ever, visionary power is needed today, in developing new political strategies. For strategic planning, the innovative forces of high-level scientific and technological development will be factors of great importance.

I am, of course, speaking against the background of my experience in Sweden. But I know — and this meeting has shown — that this experience is basically common to all our countries.

In the general debate on university — industry interaction it has, by tradition, been the demands of industry on the educational system that come into the foreground. The flow of skilled personnel from institutions of higher education into enterprise is certainly the basic mechanism for university-industry relations. The importance of the competence and skill of the individual was rightly stressed already at the outset of this meeting by Curt Nicolin. We know that in most OECD countries, and not least in Sweden, much effort has gone into further orientation of the educational systems to the needs of the labor market. Also in research planning, the demands of the industrial sector have increasingly been reflected.

Traditionally, a large part of technological development in Sweden has been per-

Ingvar Carlsson is Deputy Prime Minister of Sweden.

formed and financed by the enterprise sector, whereas the industrial share of basic research has been low, compared to other OECD countries. This, of course, has made the actual transfer from public research to industrial development dependent upon close and efficient cooperation between the two sectors.

The relationships are now becoming more complex, and, I believe, we are approaching a stage where there will be an added shared of responsibility on the industrial side.

"The Key to Survival"

In recent years, Swedish industry, in deciding its investment priorities, has placed an even greater emphasis on R&D, aware that "knowledge is the key to survival," to use George Bugliarello's words. This commits our university institutions to an increasing extent to applied research, which is financed and formulated by external sources. The possibilities, as well as dangers, for universities inherent in such a development have been treated at length during these discussions. The conclusions that I wish to draw, as a politician, are the following: we must continue to improve the possibilities of cooperation between industrial development and publicly funded research; we must, above all, strengthen the capabilities of our universities in performing basic research; *and* we must coordinate industrial and technological policies, aiming at clearer relationships, but also at a sharing of responsibility between the enterprise and public sectors.

Much, for instance, has been said in the Swedish debate recently about the bureaucracy of the university sector, a problem for which we are now trying to find a solution. We cannot afford in the present situation to waste human and economic resources on administrative procedures. But the problem of efficiency in technological transfer is not confined to the actors in the public sector; it will be seen in the industrial partner as well. Also on the receiving side, rigid structures of planning and decision-making will prevent potential innovations emanating from university laboratories to break through the barriers.

We need basic knowledge produced by research in the various disciplines. We need the skills to apply this knowledge, and to communicate it between the scientist and people in practical action. And we need to continuously update knowledge and skills.

Like others before him, Ingvar Seregard today again stressed the importance of competence. The development of competence is a goal that different actors share in common: competence to develop the innovative capacity of industry, competence to stimulate the vitality of university R&D, and competence to promote national economic development. High-quality research at universities and research institutes, and high-quality industrial development work are prerequisites for one another. In Sweden, as is illustrated by the arrangements of this conference, this view is shared by all parties, and by the organizations of the labor market, as well as by political decision-makers.

The responsibilities and opportunities of the different actors on the university-industry stage have penetrated the recommendations which have been put forward. Even though some of the issues I have raised are dependent on national factors, the level of the problems, in general, is such that ideas may well be shared and solutions found in international cooperation.

Indeed — we are interdependent as countries, just as the different sectors are on a national level. For the technological development of a small nation like Sweden, international relations have always been vital, and always will be.

The Role of Industry

H.L. Beckers

There has been a lot of talk about relationships between small companies and universities, and rightly so. But, as a representative of one of the bigger industrial companies, I would like to address this subject of university-industry interactions. After all, there are still a few around.

Economic development is obviously an aim of industry, whether by the promotion and use of technical competence or otherwise (say, by marketing and planning techniques) does not really matter. The fact is that, as the scientific world comes up with new insights, the community at large — including industry — will start to apply these new insights in due course. Perhaps economic activity — including a war — stimulates scientific development; perhaps it is the other way around. I guess it is one of those chicken-and-egg questions.

Let's think of another question, and ask ourselves: "What comes first, invention or science?" Whatever your answer is you will find at least one distinguished gentleman on your side.

If you think invention comes first, you will find Professor Michie agreeing with you. Recently he started a lecture on machine intelligence with the words:

At the time of the Kitty Hawk flight, there was no science of aerodynamics (14–17 February 1983).

If you think science comes first, you will find my opposite number in Exxon, Dr. David, on your side. Talking the other day about the corporate role in basic energy research, he said:

In the end, the Wright brothers succeeded where others failed because they studied aerodynamics (12 January 1983).

Since we are all scientists or ex-scientists here, I am sure you would like to know which is the correct statement, Prof. Michie's or Dr. David's. To find the answer I asked a German Professor of Aerodynamics at the Technological University of Delft in the Netherlands whether or not the inventors of the aeroplane, the Wright brothers, had studied aerodynamics. His answer was:

Of course they did. Aerodynamics existed thirty years before the aeroplane. But the Wright brothers were not the first. My countryman Lilienthal was the first to study the practical application of aerodynamics.

H.L. Beckers is Group Research Coordinator for Shell International and President-elect of EIRMA (European Industrial Research Management Association).

Now what may we conclude from this preamble?

- First of all, Research Directors of Oil Companies are always right.
- Second, people first draw up a thesis and then try to find proof for that thesis afterwards. Mind you, there is nothing wrong with that, and we all do it. For example, looking back at what Kepler did when he formulated his famous laws on the movement of the planets, one finds that the scanty and inaccurate data he found gave no clue of an elliptical trajectory. He must have started out with the pieces and with the thesis; after that the data fell into place.
- The third and last conclusion which we can draw — and this brings us back to our main theme, university–industry relations — is that both Michie and David are aware of the fact that science and invention play leapfrog. They take turns in jumping over each other on the road to progress. Dr. Michie, as a university professor, feels the invention of knowledge machines should be followed by a machine-oriented theory of knowledge. That happens to be his speciality. As an industrial research director, Dr. David knows that, as he puts it, "basic research is what puts the white rabbit into the magician's hat."

The Leap-Frog Phenomenon

As I said in the beginning, it is probably a chicken-and-egg question. The university and industry need each other to play leapfrog. If I am allowed to quote from one of my own speeches, rather than from those of others, I would like to focus on Figure 1, which I have used previously as a tribute to Professor Kistemaker, the scientist and inventor who is considered the father of the ultra-centrifuge for isotope separation.

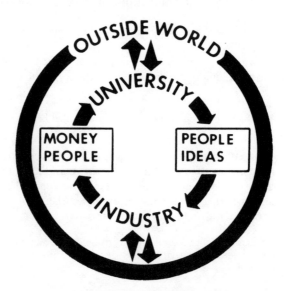

FIGURE 1. The university–industry cycle.

Figure 1 depicts what I would call the university–industry cycle. In this cycle young scientists and science are transferred from the university to industry, and mature scientists (as teachers) and money (either directly via grants or indirectly via our tax system) are flowing from industry to the university. Both academia and industry are affected by the outside world.

As you can see, if we forget about the money, the important things that are being transported across the university–industry interface are people and ideas. It is people with their ideas that leapfrog to get from one phase to the next. And just as is the case with processes like distillation and extraction, the transport across the interface is the important step.

Let us develop this leap-frogging idea through the following three points:

- The first item is "For what reason does industry do *basic* research?" I take it that we do not have to discuss the reasons why industry has to do *applied* R&D.
- The second item is *not:* "For what reason does a university do industrial research," but: "For what reason does a university do *basic* research."
- The third item then addresses areas that are suitable for cooperation between universities and industry.

I put little store in definitions of basic, exploratory or fundamental research; for convenience sake, I will call basic research, research which is oriented more towards knowledge for its own sake and less towards its application for business purposes. I should emphasize at this stage that I think that this definition of basic research includes development at the frontier of technology.

Why Basic Research?

Concerning the first question: "For what reason does industry do basic research?" I would like to discuss three answers:

- to facilitate recruiting;
- to provide a window on the world; and
- to support applied R&D.

By the way, you will appreciate that when I use the term industry, I am speaking on the basis of my experience with the Royal Dutch/Shell Group to which I myself belong. However, I believe that most of what I am going to say holds true for all of big and bigger industry, even though big industry encompasses birds of very different feathers—from IBM to US Steel, with the oil companies somewhere in between.

The first reason for my industry to do basic research is that it helps us to recruit the people we need. Shell measures its potential employees against a number of standards, of which technical scientific excellence certainly is not the least. The only way these budding scientists have of making a choice between different industrial laboratories is by using technological and scientific yardsticks. The young scientists and engineers want to apply what they have been taught, or they are looking for ways to learn more while making themselves useful at the same time. The basic research departments of industrial laboratories are often a very convenient link between school and industry.

The second reason is that it provides a window on the world. The basic science division functions as a radar antenna. It scans the world for new, significant scientific findings. The division itself should be working at the forefront of scientific development to be able to identify the key issues in science and technology. The fact that it *is* at the forefront makes it a worthwhile sounding board for people at the university who want a partner to discuss their ideas with. Thus the basic science division in industry at the same time provides the university with a touchstone and its employer with an alert system, and it is all based on interactions between people.

The third reason is to support applied research and development. Applied R&D is aimed more towards application for business purposes and less towards knowledge for its own sake. What we hope for in industry is, of course, that our basic research will not pay off in terms of recruiting top scientists and alerting us to new scientific insights, but that our basic research will provide us with new ideas to improve our processes and products. While waiting for that to happen and also to let the basic researchers know what the needs of our industry really are, we encourage our applied scientists to discuss their problems with their basic friends.

Just between you and me, this also allows the basic researcher to keep a beady eye trained on any happy inventor who tries to fly by flapping his feather-covered arms rather than by studying aerodynamics.

The Role of the University in Basic Research

When I was writing this speech I had a sneaking suspicion that what Herbert Fusfeld wanted me to do at this stage was to discuss reasons why a university should do more industrial-oriented R&D. However, that is not what I will do; instead I would like to discuss why a university *ought* to do basic research, which as you may recall I defined as research which is aimed at the production of knowledge.

In my opinion there are three main answers: first, to create the next generation of scientists, among which are our recruits; second, to prepare the ground for new inventions; and, third, to give the university credibility as an impartial judge on possible side effects of the new inventions.

As illustrated in the figure on the university-industry cycle, it is people and ideas that link universities and industry. The people that industry needs are people who have been trained to do science, not people who have been trained to do what they are told to do.

I am reminded of a practice which existed in colonial times. The scientific training of the natives in some part of the world consisted of calculating square roots by hand. Eventually they became extremely well versed in doing that, and also in doing minutely and accurately what they were told to do. These natives were not taught how to advance science or how to apply scientific means in novel ways. Whenever a real problem presented itself, an expert had to be shipped from Europe to solve it.

We in industry do not want trained "natives." We need the real experts, who can solve new problems and propose novel avenues. These experts are not formed by letting them ruminate on known industrial problems. Industry can chew its own cud! What we need in our industrial laboratories are people who have not only been taught science, and how to apply it, but who have also been taught how to advance science. And in my mind the only way to learn how to move the boundaries of our knowledge outwards is to be active at the forefront of scientific development, that is, in basic science and at the limits of technology.

The Father of Invention

Often people forget that invention, whose mother is called necessity, also has a father. Of course, the ovum is much larger than the spermatozoon, but one cannot have a mother without a father. The father of invention, as we saw in the beginning of my talk, is called science. This brings us to the second reason why a university should do basic research.

Research at the university should be an exploration into the unknown with no more than a passing thought to the ultimate utilization of the findings. I don't think that De Laval, who is considered to be one of the founders of aerodynamics, had an inkling of what Lilienthal and the Wright brothers would do in 130 years' time.

In basic research the only thing that counts is the quality of the research: Necessity in due course will bear the application. The university should choose its area for search on the basis of its own assessment of what its strengths really are. Universities should not aim to be in phase with industrial research – the industrial laboratories can, or should be able to take care of their own. Let me repeat that the *aim* of research in academia should not be industrial application. Obviously, if a university professor finds an application to be the logical next step in the course of work, that step should not be shunned. And, if an engineering school or university with a particularly useful kind of expertise would offer me in industry a helping hand, I obviously would take that hand.

But the cooperation should be sheer serendipity. The university should not force itself to fall in line with industrial needs. If a university followed that course, it would soon find itself addressing shorter-and-shorter-term problems.

The third reason for a university to do basic research – which it should do without regard for perceived industrial needs – is that it should be, and should be seen to be, an impartial judge of progress. In this capacity it should strive to educate opinion makers and, if needed, the public at large, as well as the bright starry-eyed young student. Let me give an example. Some ten years ago there was a public outcry against research in recombinant DNA. The intensity of the resistance varied from country to country. In The Netherlands, for instance, some Dutch industries had to farm out their R&D outside The Netherlands. I do not think that industry would have been able to remove the fears of a Frankenstein producing monstrous bacteria trained to kill human life on the planet earth. To remove these unfounded fears, society needs a credible authority, and the university is admirably suited for that role as long as it is, and is seen to be, independent of industry and not too dependent on industrial funds. A university should have no other axe to grind than to further the understanding of nature and human artifacts and to disseminate its impartial findings.

Scope for Cooperation

From what I have said so far about the independent and, at the same time, interdependent functions of academia and industry, you may wonder whether there is any scope for cooperation left. Actually, there is. I will try to make a split in our industrial R&D programs to facilitate the discussion.

We can distinguish three areas, which I have called, without trying to be too precise,

- non-competitive scientific knowledge,
- long-term R&D programs, and
- competitive scientific knowledge.

The first area, that of noncompetitive scientific knowledge, concerns research where we simply want to be current with leaders in the field, but where we cannot expect to derive a crucial advantage from proprietary knowledge. Examples in the oil industry would include:

- plate tectonics to assist the search for oil;
- explanatory studies on catalysis to support the development of conversion processes; and
- combustion science and tribology as the basis for studies on engine fuels and lubricants.

In these fields we want a strong in-house expertise, but much of the work could be carried out in higher education institutions, if they possess the requisite know-how.

The next area where there is scope for useful cooperation is related to longer term R&D programs. Here we keep in touch with ideas in the world which could lead to new technologies. The recombinant DNA technique, which I mentioned a while ago, might serve as an example. Industry does not have the resources to keep all the options open, and we are anxious to undertake cooperative work. This cooperation, of course, should be advantageous to both parties. In the category of noncompetitive knowledge, the scope and depth of the cooperation is almost without limit; in the category of long-term R&D, industry seeks a competitive advantage, and the cooperation has to be more circumscribed and business-like. But, at the same time, the university should preserve its independent status, in view of what I said earlier about the role of the university as a referee.

In the third area, that of competitive research, cooperation between industry and university is rather unusual. Here industry is seeking a crucial advantage from proprietary knowledge.

Quite often we are talking about established areas of technology: in Shell's case, for example, oil refining, where the interplay of technology, market, economic, and even political factors is complex and changing. In these areas the contribution that higher education institutes can make is of a background or peripheral nature only.

I do hope that I have not disappointed my friends in academia by not encouraging them to enter a number of avenues which they may have thought would lead to cooperation. On the other hand, I hope that I have encouraged them to continue on the road of academic freedom.

Summary

I see mainly two roles for the university, one is as an institution that provides higher education. Any arrangements with industry on research and development should be supportive of that role and not destructive or subversive. You cannot go far wrong in this, if—in considering whether or not to start industry-oriented R&D—you ask yourself the question: "Does this support and enhance our ability to turn out well educated students?" If the answer to this is: "No," I would suggest you think again.

The second role is as a generator of new knowledge, whether in science or in technology. Industry and university need each other, as they exchange people and leapfrog from scientific discovery to invention to scientific discovery, as aerodynamics made the flying machine possible and aerodynamics blossomed through the flying machine. But, at the same time, the university should continue its random walk in search for truth and knowledge, if we ever are to get beyond emerging antiquities like chips, genetic engineering, and fusion.

The Role of The University

Guy Denielou

If I have understood well what has been said here, the university has no choice: either it remains a cold virgin locked in some ivory tower, or it indulges in prostitution. (With some perversity one could even imagine that that prostitution may take place inside the ivory tower.)

Everybody, from Namibia to the UK and from China to Belgium, is complaining about the poor relationship between universities and industry. If we wish here to do something about it, we must first of all clearly understand *why there is a need for relationship* — or improved relationship — between the two.

The world has been undergoing a profound change since the end of World War II. This change is comparable in magnitude only to the birth of agriculture some 9,000 years ago. For the first time, man's environment is no longer nature, but man-made objects: that is, culture. The geological impact of man on earth is no longer negligible. Installed power plants have a total capacity which is comparable to tidal power: we are as powerful as the moon!

The social impact of science and technology has become the main factor in our evolution. Technology, the scientific approach to our products and processes, has replaced techniques and knowhow. Almost everything can now be amenable to calculus; 50 years ago almost nothing could be calculated. This revolution happened in a very short span. May I recall that I have been in charge of the Research and Development program of fast breeder reactors in France (Rapsodie, Phénix, . . .). But when I was a boy, my good grandmother used to tell me not to play by the windmills, because they were so dangerous. Remember that the windmills were probably found by the people of Harapa, near the Indus Valley, maybe 1,500 years before Christ.

We have a tendency to underestimate the rapidity of the technological revolution. Our university system is very old; it came out of a long trial and error process and is not suited to the new era. Clearly, we must analyze why.

The first answer is that there is a complete contradiction, (of the type that Chinese people call *Mao Toun,* that is, irreducible contradiction) between to *know* and to *do.* You may add up all knowledge, but it is not going to result in any action. You may add up all actions, but no knowledge will come out of it. There is an orthogonality between the many disciplines of science and the many branches of engineering. One must bear in mind the resulting matrix. The problem is that, since the advent of technology, no intersection between line and column in this

Guy Denielou is President of the University of Technology at Compiègne.

matrix is empty. Today each science becomes useful to all industries; every industry has a need for all sciences.

One cannot think of this contradiction as purely static. People used to the methods of science and devoted to knowledge quickly lose their aptitude for action and even their capacity for understanding the rules of the game and the laws of industry. On the other hand, people engaged in companies, in plants, in projects, and in planning lose their ability to understand the internal necessities of science. Besides, we have a tendency to think of the past as though this type of problem had been solved by our fathers. In fact, it was not solved, because they did not have the problem. Industry developed largely independently of science. Pasteurization was found probably 50 years before Pasteur on purely empirical grounds. Riveting machines were invented in the 19th century without (or almost without) any help from scientists.

Increasing Knowledge

A second answer can be found in the fact that our education is an integration process. Today we require from universities and schools that they act as derivation operators. Knowledge was supposed to be some kind of accumulation. What was found true by our ancestors remained so today. But—as the frontiers of science expanded—the total quantity, if I may say so, of knowledge increased. The role of the university was, indeed, to contribute to the expansion, but also to organize the field, to put some order and synthesis in the mass of facts and theories and, of course, to transmit this treasure to youth. This introduced a time constant in some transfer function; the old people knew best and knew more than the young. The image of the scientist was old and bearded.

Today the young are good in computer science; the old have some fear of the keyboard. People expect from scientists and the university that they can cast some light on the future. They expect them to contribute to making the future. Our education system is supposed to be able to prepare tomorrow's world. This is a new situation. We are not used to it. The future is no longer what it used to be.

A third answer is that techniques do not have a good reputation in universities. Objects and products are not as popular as concepts and ideas. But how could science and the university be of some social relevance in a technological society if they remain far from the objects?

Last year, in Stockholm, we tried to underline how the university–industry relationship was easier when both sides met close to some material object. We did show that there was a tendency in companies to escape in the direction of finance, just as there was a temptation in the university to escape in the direction of mathematics. In both cases there was a substitution of written symbols to hard facts. On the other hand, when you have a discussion around a pump or around a fuel-element sub-assembly, the object itself serves as a medium and allows communication between the scientist and engineer.

Today, I would try a new approach or make a new proposal to improve the dialogue between the two opposite parts.

Why not think of universities and schools as being companies or plants? Of course, their production is included in what is called the "tertiary" sector, *i.e.*, their product is largely not material: research and teaching can be thought of as service, just like banking or tour-operating. In fact, is that not already the case? Don't we often refer to the people with whom we have research contracts as "our customer"? Don't we often say that we are going to "sell" to industry the idea of some new "major" or some other "minor"? Science is no longer a hobby for people rich enough to own a physics closet. Higher education is no longer a cultural affair for the young whose fathers can afford it.

Why do we manufacture and sell the two products of the university in one and the same plant? Is it not for economic reasons? Is it because overhead can be reduced by this trick? Because the student is often very qualified for research and underpaid? And because he is pleased to do it? Is it not true that, by linking teaching and research, we are able to solve the dilemma between integration and derivation? Being close to research, teaching can be more readily modified and can follow the pace of progress.

The Teaching Product

Let us look more deeply into the teaching product. Any teacher is faced with a choice of becoming a professor or a pedagogue. In the first case, he is interested in the coherence of his teaching, in the elegance of the proof, in the perfection of demonstration, and so forth. If he is a pedagogue, he is interested mainly in the success of the young engineer he is supervising. Instead of trying to reproduce in his pupil the image of himself, he tries to satisfy the requirements of a market. Is not the second way more promising because it is more economic?

How is the pedagogue going to know what the requirement of the market is? Of course, he may ask people in industry. But he must be very careful in using this sort of elementary market polling, because usually people in industry have no long-term views. They are prepared to answer what they feel you expect them to answer. They will give you a description of the future engineer as a Nobel Prize, a heavyweight W.B.C. world champion, a good psychologist, and a wonderful leader. The pedagogue must himself decipher the long-term trends in industry. He has to balance programs accordingly. Of course, he must not be interested only in program and curriculum. He knows that the five years spent in the universities are of paramount importance for the character formation of the young, that it is in the university that they can develop entrepreneurship, realism, and exactitude. If the university is itself a well managed company, then it will be the place where students become good engineers. We could give more instances.

Let us have a look now at the research product. There is usually some contradiction between so-called fundamental research and applied research. How does this contradiction look in the light of our approach?

Research is expensive. Research for small companies is just as difficult as is research for big companies. Small companies usually cannot afford it, if they pay the going price. If they cannot afford it, the university cannot sell them this type of product. The only possible way is then to sell the same research to several companies. Of course, you cannot do that to several companies competing in the same field (maybe you can do it once, but, after that, you would no longer have a chance). You must, therefore, sell the same research to several companies working in different fields, such as one in biomedicine, one in meteorology, and one in nuclear engineering. Such research is called fundamental research. It is fundamental because it can be sold several times to several customers.

Another point: if your university is a company, it will be easier to gather around it several small firms, usually in advanced technology. On the other hand, the intimate knowledge of the functioning of such firms will help you in your dialogue in industry. Here again, we could develop many other examples. In conclusion, thinking of a university as a company helps develop a common spirit and a common image. It helps to give unity to the university. Far from being deleterious to academic freedom, this unity seems to be the very condition of survival of the university.

It reminds me of a cartoon where you see students picketing under the word "Unity." A student asks a co-ed: "I always forget. Are we uniting against or are we uniting for?" Today, many faculties are more prone to unite against, in order to protect their discipline, their personal independence, or even their privileges. I think they are the losers. The future belongs to those who will be capable of uniting *for,* within the framework of a strong university with its policy, its marketing, its customers, its image, its global budget, etc.: that is a company.

The Role of Scientists and Engineers

Ingvar Seregard

When called upon to address an international forum on a subject like this, it seems natural to express my views from the standpoint of my day-to-day work, which is that of a trade union leader.

In Sweden, we have a law designed to promote joint participation in the decision-making process at the workplace, commonly referred to as the Codetermination Act. This legislation has been on the statute books for some years and has received a measure of criticism in several respects. But the labor market has negotiated a codetermination agreement within the framework of the same legislation. This negotiated agreement will provide a wide range of opportunities for progress in exploiting fresh knowledge for the development of our economy. This is not, however, the sole reason why the two sides elected to refer to it as a development agreement.

By the terms of this agreement, employees have committed themselves to assuming a greater degree of responsibility in participating in the decision process. Obviously, this responsibility is not limited merely to the making of decisions, but also extends to participation in ensuring that decisions are based on the best grounds available. The ability of development agreement to fulfill its function in this respect will be contingent on the cooperation of both sides in a process where top priority is assigned to the acquisition and implementation of fresh knowledge and skills.

In the context of putting the fruits of scientific research, new technologies, new work methods, and so on to work in promoting a rational and competitive economy, I believe that the organization of our trade unions in Sweden — with many professions in the same union, and the unions' positive attitude towards rationalization — has made an invaluable contribution to this process. Furthermore, the trade union organizations have found little difficulty in participating in an ongoing process of rationalization when the changes necessitated by the process could be implemented during periods of full employment.

At present, these difficulties are growing in the wake of a decline in employment. Nevertheless, we can still discern a generally favorable attitude on the part of the trade unions towards a continued process of rationalization. I will not attempt a more detailed analysis of the motives for this attitude, but I feel that it is worth drawing your attention to the different behavior of some trade unions in many

Ingvar Seregard is President of the Federation of Salaried Employees in Industry and Services (PTK), and Vice Chairman of Trygghetsrädet SAF-PTK, Sweden.

other countries when faced with this situation. That is why I believe that it is important that the continued development of our economy should take place in an atmosphere of direct and active cooperation between management and all employees.

However, I believe that we have witnessed a growing polarization in recent years, primarily between representatives of the employers and the trade unions. The clash on the subject of the "wage-earner funds" has clearly played a major role in the evolution of this situation, although I am not entirely convinced that it is the sole reason. Nor should we close our eyes to the threat of growing polarization between representatives of the employers and the salaried staff unions for reasons outside the political sphere. There are also some signs of a threat of polarizations in opinion between different categories of employees. Of course, it is in the general interest of the country as a whole that we all do our best to avoid any further increase in this situation. But I am sorry to say that I am not so sure that this is possible.

Financial Aid

In the trade union movement we have good reason to scrutinize the nature of our participation in different programs of financial aid. It is not merely a matter of the effect such programs have in protecting the livelihood of our individual members. We must also consider the overall picture of the manner in which we utilize available manpower in relation to the manufacturing base that we can reasonably be expected to achieve in Sweden. Insisting in each instance that the factories must set up operations where manpower is available and not vice versa is an economic impossibility if we are to continue to support a reasonably high standard of living.

I would like to draw attention to what I consider an important acquisition of knowledge in the context of our statement on the lack of flexibility on the part of employers, at companies, and among the work force. Growing pressure on our ability to readjust quickly to market conditions is triggering an increasing demand for extension training and further education. Some of the large companies are undoubtedly well to the fore in this field and participate in systematic extension training programs for their personnel.

However, most companies do not look very favorably on further education that requires long periods of absence from the company. It is probably only natural that their first consideration is for the needs of the present. But I believe that it is important to the company as well as to its employees—and will be even more important in the future—to organize a systematic and regular program of future education on a more in-depth basis than the isolated one-week course now and then. I regard the implementation of more extension training and further education for the work force as a vehicle that will also serve to promote greater understanding among employees of the necessity of readjustment. The greater scope in purely practical opportunities that more training offers a company for the implementation of rapid readjustment to market conditions is a benefit I consider self-evident.

The very size of the amount of information with which we are flooded today poses a serious problem to engineers and other employees, and we are finding it increasingly difficult to find the information that would be of the greatest value in a given situation. We are liable to lose sight of pertinent knowledge in the current of information that we digest at a very low level of efficiency in relation to the present job in hand.

For this reason we stand to gain by improving the ability of all those seeking factual information to solve a problem in a specific field to find the information they need quickly. Both Swedish and international information retrieval systems are already available on the market, and we can expect rapid development in this field in the future. But what I believe to be our Achilles heel here in Sweden is the fact that many people who need information are unaware of the opportunities that exist today and the manner in which they can be most efficiently exploited. The provision of information and the establishment of a rational information retrieval capability constitute a very effective method of quickly making available new and pertinent information that can be transformed into a practical reality.

Knowledge in itself is of interest, as are new products, new technology, and new systems. But in the type of free market economy that we have in this country, and in the world around us in which we as a nation have to live, all new products must either reflect a demand that exists in the marketplace or a demand that can be created once the new products become known. That's why such knowledge as we seek must extend to cover the market. In this situation marketing departments have assumed growing importance in most companies. It is not, however, merely a matter of selling today's products on the market. Studying the needs for the market in terms of future products and identifying a suitable niche for the company are equally important.

Only a few of the biggest Swedish companies have the resources to establish their own sales and marketing organization on an international basis. Some of the knowledge and understanding of international markets that must be fed back to Swedish industry and the Swedish economy can, of course, be obtained through the services of our technical attachés, through study visits, and through the interchange of information at the international level. But I believe that we could achieve a better degree of coordination in the flow of information to small- and medium-sized companies by fostering a greater degree of cooperation between companies and, in some cases, by establishing more direct and extensive channels of communications between industry and the community.

Facing the Consequences

Obviously, if we insist on high standards of quality and a respectable order of magnitude in research work in a country as small as ours with its limited resources, the consequences will have to be faced. We must exercise special care in our consideration of the mechanics of the procedures that lead to the selection of suitable subjects for research, as well as the entire educational systems through which our researchers pass. Without wishing to pass judgment on how successful our community has been in solving this task, I would like to emphasize how important it is for our political decision-makers to treat these issues in the light of long-term considerations. This would apply to the adoption of programs of educational reform, and improved economic prospects for young people during their years of study, as well as to financial and other incentives designed to promote confidence in the future of scientific research.

I think that all of us would endorse the idealistic requirement for the independence of scientific research. A small, but highly industrialized country, such as Sweden needs, however, to assign priorities to its research resources. Our efforts must be directed towards investing the most money in areas where we believe we will be able to make the most attractive new discoveries. We will, of course, still have a pretty large spread of investment in different areas of research in a pluralistic society such as ours.

My personal preference in the allocation of greater priority leans towards areas of technology that are already emerging as attractive commercial propositions and are expected to expand very rapidly over the coming decade — electrical engineering, electronics, and genetic research, for instance. By directing the main thrust of our limited financial resources towards these and similar fields, we will surely create far better opportunities for exchanging the fruits of our research work with those of other highly industrialized countries. We would, so to speak, develop into a more attractive partner for such exchanges. Our material prosperity has always been dependent on knowledge created in other countries and I believe that an intensive exchange of scientific knowledge is essential, if we are to stay in the running and make some contribution to developments on a global scale for the benefit of all mankind.

The Transfer of Knowledge

While on the subject of our dependence on knowledge created in other countries, I would like to draw your attention to the manner in which knowledge in some countries is generated from scientific research and promptly transferred to commercially viable products for launching on different markets. I believe that we have quite a lot to learn in this respect.

We must try to find new avenues of approach for establishing cooperation between researchers in state-run institutes and researchers, engineers, and others engaged in the task of getting the fruits of basic research out of the laboratory and into the commercial market in the form of viable products and systems. If this cannot be done under the existing terms and conditions of employment, perhaps we could achieve a better level of cooperation by having industry and the community join forces to set up special institutes, and by enabling research scientists to obtain leaves of absence from government service for specific periods to allow them to participate with a greater degree of latitude in developments that will prove of direct benefit to the economy and all of us in general.

Currently, there is talk of transferring part of the Royal Institute of Technology in Stockholm to a site to the north of the city in an area where a large number of electronics companies have set up business. I believe that this is a correct approach, provided that ways can be found to establish suitable forms of cooperation between research scientists at the Royal Institute of Technology and the private companies as well as between companies engaged in closely related fields.

In other countries, we have seen how many universities have adopted suitable forms of cooperation and successfully fostered an industrial climate in their immediate vicinity that has proved of enormous benefit to progress in the fields of advanced technologies. This approach has engendered the emergence of a number of very vigorous companies. And there certainly are plenty of fields where the establishment of a suitable form of cooperation between universities and industry would be capable of creating very fertile soil for the growth of high-technology companies in the immediate vicinity of the university.

If we are to arrest the continued decline in our standard of living and lay the foundations for improving our material standard in the future, we must invest in knowledge and advanced technology products. To sum up, I would like to point out that this will require prompt access to pertinent facts in many fields of technology in the face of all product development. This will also require a commercial understanding of the current and future needs of the market. This in turn will require cooperation between research scientists in institutes of higher learning and industry, and between company management, salaried workers, and wage earners. Much creativity will continue to derive from systematic research and development work conducted by the major companies. But international experience has shown that new high-technology companies can be created using suitable forms and conditions of cooperation and enterprise. In most cases, such companies expand far more rapidly than the older, more institutionalized companies. That is why I am a proponent of cooperation and united action on a broad front, even on issues where — at any rate in the past — we have not been so accustomed to cooperate.

This conference has touched on issues of crucial importance to employment and the industrial economy in Sweden, and I am convinced that it will serve to provide us with an added stimulus for the implementation of a number of different action programs. One logical consequence would be the holding of a follow-up conference with emphasis on Swedish conditions and with an agenda that devotes sufficient space to the consideration of the organizational and economic problems related to the dynamism in our "system of skills." We hope that it will be possible for a conference of this type to be arranged in the autumn by the Royal Swedish Academy of Engineering Scientists (IVA) in cooperation with the Swedish Board for Technical Development (STU), the Swedish Association of Graduate Engineers (CF), and the Employment Security Council (TRR).

Other activities planned in consultation with these and other organizations include a detailed study of what skills must be represented, different aspects in relation to divergent fields of activity, and different organizational structures — in other words, spanning the whole spectrum from knowledge and proficiency in the application of knowledge to motivation, to the ability to communicate, and to the framework of cooperation and management of a project.

Actions to Strengthen University–Industry Cooperation

Duncan Davies

Well into a long meeting, appetite for detail and sophisticated argument becomes jaded. So I have tabulated a number of headlines about "things to do" that have emerged during the discussions, and added one or two of my own. Most of them aren't about technology or research, and some of them may sound dull and tedious. All are important. Alongside each, I've indicated the relevant skill.

- Accentuating the Positive and Ignoring the Unhelpful Majority (psychology)
- Understanding the Drives and Constraints: Living Together: Pursuing the Counter-Cultural (behavior)
- Selecting, Rejecting, and Phasing (management)
- Learning from Others (technology transfer)
- Making Things Work and Sell Well (quality standards)
- Raising the Patient Long-term Money (finance)
- Creating the Right Agencies: Technology Parks: Takeover Procedure (politics)

Perhaps the most important feature of this list is that it is unheroic. There is some tendency for everyone to overemphasize major innovations, simply because they are spectacular. Universitites have played a key part in important innovations. Here is an incomplete list of innovations in the UK:

Medical	Computing	Electronic Instruments
cephalosporin	memory computers (Atlas)	stereoscan microscope
contraceptive pill	networking	liquid crystal display
ultrasonic diagnosis	high-level language	

The important point is that the university role has often been to devise an instrument, or show how to model a disease, or provide infrastructure. And most major primary innovations do not involve universities because they require skills — *e.g.,* those of knowing about actual and possible markets — that are well outside university subject areas. Yet this in no way detracts from the importance of the subject of this conference; national well-being depends more on scientific optimization

Duncan Davies is Chairman and Consulting Director of BCRA, Ltd. He is the former Chief Scientist and Engineer, Department of Industry, United Kingdom.

and the widely diffused application of science to procedures, costs, and quality than on the celebrated and over-lauded "breakthrough."

I have now assembled some possible actions, as suggested during the meeting, under each headline. Additionally, it is helpful to take note of the kind of input represented in this case. I have used three index letters:

- O = Original, "odd-ball"; the kind that can help lead to primary innovation, or something done for the first time. Examples have been given above.
- C = Generation of consensus for cooperation within the organization, such as is needed for secondary innovation (no less important than primary). This is the action that leads to products of greater reliability, quality, or design, or to improved and more economic processes.
- S = Sharing or transfer between organizations; the general benefit that can come from the diffusion of ideas, methods, or technology.

Accentuating the Positive and Ignoring the Unhelpful Majority

- "Clubs," to share project results when possible, transfer technology, and develop local and regional strengths (S);
- Introductions to others who can help, perhaps from an unusual angle (O);
- Meetings, bulletins, videotapes (O,C,S);
- Protection of liaison officers (job rotation?) (C,S); and
- All methods for generating confidence (O,C,S).

A report on this subject ten years ago by Pat Docksey has the headline, "stop nagging." It was right, but in this world of sighs, I am afraid that some industrial people would tend to speak of university folk as unrealistic layabouts and some university people speak of industrialists as stupid and shortsighted moneygrubbers. It may be some further thousands of years before this background noise is stilled; all of us are going to go on living in a world where there are plenty of potential university–industry collaborators, all of whom are going to endure opprobrium— especially during hard times—for their counter-cultural temerity. What matters is that there should be steady propaganda for the successes and tolerance of the inevitable failures, which the unhelpful majority will cite as instances of the normal expectation. This propaganda for the positive is not easy, for all the participants— again, especially in hard times—tend to exaggerate their own contributions. But I would particularly support Dr. Nicolin's plea for the generation of confidence in all possible ways. Both in firms and universities, times are tough. Those with ideas and successes can gain strength from one another.

We also need to communicate broadly and efficiently; here, the use of video tapes can help greatly. Technical reporting is not easy to read, and has little general impact. Video can have far more, and is judged by the more stringent standards on TV.

We must protect the "liaison offices" whose incumbents have a somewhat thankless task. Whether industry or university, their support fluctuates widely, and the threat of closure is never far away. Permanent officers become stale (and occasionally may have been put there "because they could be spared"). Ideally, this should be a secondment job, sought after because of the contacts and the broad view that it brings. Can we do more in this direction?

Understanding the Drives and Constraints: Living Together (behavior)

- Joint projects going beyond R&D (C);
- Brainstorming (O);
- Finding small sums for wild ideas: bootlegging (O);
- Joint work in the operation of funding agencies (S);
- Pre-competitive work in clubs (S);
- Teaching the basis for enterprise (O,C);
- "Incubation centers" (O,C);
- Teaching exercises based on "computer-based instruction" (O,C); and
- Open universities (*e.g.,* UK) (O,C,S).

In industry, it is very exhausting to be a generator of new ideas, most of which will fail the tests of marketability or possibility of consensus. In universities, it is very exhausting to try to be realistic about markets; the expectation is that a clever notion or product will, somehow, be saleable at a profit. If the proposition is turned down, or fails, the usual response is "not fair" or "incompetent development."

It is therefore, very important for actions to be taken whereby:

- industrial managers become inclined to be adventurous and dedicated in seeking to develop counter-cultural products, processes, and technology from universities and elsewhere;
- university teachers and researchers become more realistic in accepting that the disciplines of the market are exacting, and, often legitimately, rule out exciting and clever innovative ideas; and
- both recognize the vital part to be played by both agencies together.

This can be summed up under the heading "arrangements for cohabitation." It is simply impossible to establish this mutual understanding by preaching or lecturing to one another, or by advocacy of an instant, courtroom variety. I return to special kinds of agencies, such as technology parks, but even without these, much can be done. One successful practice in Japan, for example, is the creation, with government, of jointly-funded consortia, held together by a formal commitment and scheme, but with no new premises or organizations. Such arrangements can pursue a new technology through the "pre-competitive" phase.

Another practice is for government to encourage one-off partnerships between a firm and a university on a topic with too long a range for the firm to finance. The UK Industry Requirements Boards and the German BMFT keep sponsoring groups together for such partnership promotion regulation. Research councils can set aside some of their funds for encouraging marriages, and government laboratories (*e.g.,* the USNBS) can take helpful initiatives. There are many recipes, and the need is for formal commitment and persistence, with some inevitable bureaucracy. There are good schemes in Sweden.

Perhaps the most important message from our conference is that there can be, and is, great variety of approach. In Japan, university funding is done without heavy intrusion in project selection: that occurs as part of the job. In Europe, the collaborators more often are brought together at the point when funding is decided. Both methods have their strengths and drawbacks. There is, therefore, a strong case for keeping a watch for methods that work. At present, such agencies as the Massachusetts High Technology Council seem to be doing a great deal to develop real strength, and the UK Open University creates a variety of patterns of cooperation.

Selecting, Rejecting, Phasing

- Agencies to share the decision process (C,S);
- Joint work on timetables and phasing (C,S).
- Joint strategies with scope for brilliant oddity (O,S); and
- Good tactical moves within strategies (takeover, etc.) (C,S).

This is an extension of "Accentuating the Positive" and is concerned with the need for strategic design as well as tactical choice. Many ideas are tabled, and not all can be chosen. Simple "window shopping" very soon runs up against vociferous children getting the most goods, and in all but the biggest economies the degree of selection must be great, so that reasonably clear ideas about the top priorities are needed. Even if these, later, are seen to have been chosen sub-optimally, they are still needed. Anarchy is harmful and divisive.

Firms have to be arbiters of practicality, for they have to do the post-development selling and improvement, without which hard-won market share is lost. Some of their money must be called for right from the start, or commitment is lacking. The world is full of 100% taxpayer-funded projects that have been quite well done, but to whose follow-up no one is committed. A decision to fund — even to the tune of only 10% or 20% — is a serious decision to persist, for no one puts in money mindlessly. Shared funding makes initial advocacy of counter-cultural ideas more difficult, but it is best to have the arguments at this stage.

When there is an effective strategy body, it can select in imaginative ways. Some fields must be attacked now or not all; others are best taken steadily, bio-technology, for example. Others, such as satellites, require a "minimum entry fee" below which the effort is ineffective. Accordingly a government-led body with strategy as well as tactics can devote some of the money to quick assaults and some to long hauls. This makes it possible to devote some attention, at all times, to really adventurous ideas. But never enough for the ideas men, some of whom will inevitably be walking about saying that they have been robbed.

Some topics where payback is reasonably soon, say, five to ten years, are obviously suitable for venture capital. This decision area, however, is mainly suitable for products and processes that can be at least seen in outline. There are dangerous moves afoot at present, conducted by people in search of quick stock market profit, whereby venture capital is raised for vague areas, sounding interesting, but doomed by an almost inevitable loss of backing because of the long time-scale. Alongside this danger, a key benefit comes when a firm, based on stock market acquisition opportunity that fits with the firm's general strategy, takes tactical steps that then create strategic long-term commitment and opportunity. Such steps must involve the CEO as prime mover, or the staying power will be absent.

Learning from Others — Technology Transfer

- Use universities to cross-fertilize work in firms in different markets (O,S);
- Formal technology transfer schemes, embodying creation of awareness, consultancy on how to make a start, and project support, especially for small firms (C,S);
- Exchanges and cross-staffing (C,S);
- Consultancy — especially for younger staff (O,C,S); and
- "Dodging the Expert Gatekeeper" (special help from university departments in areas other than a firm's central skill — *e.g.*, chemistry for an electronics firm) (O,C,S).

It is perpetually astonishing to find how parochial we all are, and how limited is the firm-to-firm and industry-to-industry learning, unless actual sales of equipment and technical service are involved. Universities are well placed to undertake brokerage, whereby trusted people carefully bring about the transfer of nonconfidential technology. Even where exclusivity is pursued, we need to note that the whole purpose of the patent system is to ensure that good technology, protected for the time being by a patent monopoly, is known about and built on by others; and, of course, that patent monopoly is temporary.

Technology transfer agencies can be operated privately by semi-public "generic technology centers," or by universities, or by government laboratories. One powerful aid is the delineation of standards and specifications that embody good practice. When there are government schemes — such as the UK Manufacturing Advisory Service — universities should be encouraged to bid for participation as an operating center, partly financed by the taxpayer and partly by the customer. One of the principal benefits from technology transfer is the introduction of new methods into smaller firms that cannot afford their own original research, and often do not know the possible scale of the benefits. Studies of the overall economics show excellent results, often for quite modest inputs. But the private sector has difficulty in acting alone — largely because the proprietary profit is less obvious. There may be fewer new patents, and few spectacular new products that catch the headlines.

Making Things Work Well and Sell Well: Quality and Standards

- Use universities in standards-making (S); and
- Use joint bodies for quality improvement (S).

The early years of the resurgence of Japanese industrial capability in the late 1950s set the stage for the new world-renowned Japanese emphasis on quality, inspection, and fitness for purpose. As well as encouraging good design, such campaigns also encourage the standardization that enables many designers to use the same parts, thus achieving greater economies of scale in component making. The German DIN system is so effective in this that it spreads German standards to other countries and helps German exports.

There is a central problem. The initial impact of a good and stringent standards system is to increase cost and reject percentage. After this phase, better manufacturing methods can get the cost down again and produce better and more acceptable goods, at something near the original cost. This self-discipline is uncomfortable and is unlikely to be imposed by a consensus system. Universities, government, and industry have to collaborate in deciding when and to what extent this discipline can be taught, and government has to decide whether it can be backed by statute.

Raising the Patient (Long Term) Money: Finance

- Funding bodies to bring together private and public money for pre-competitive work (C,S);
- Competition for government and other funds, with publicity and prestige for winners (C,S);
- Public purchasing of suitable pioneer goods (C,S); and
- Pursue models such as the US "Council for Chemical Research" (C,S).

Much of the benefit from university–industry collaboration can be enjoyed soon enough and in easily enough recognized form for the industry partner to be able to raise the money as part of its normal funding procedure. This is true of technology transfer schemes, quality control, and standards of work, and scientifically based optimization and improvement of existing products and processes. Some innovation leading to specific and definable products and processes, too unfamiliar for orthodox finance, can be covered by venture capital. But pre-competitive technology development, and work on the general technical infrastructure is difficult to finance sustainably in this way. Unpopular as such a statement may be in some political circles, there is a key need for taxpayers' money.

Such investment, however, needs good guidance. There are innumerable candidate programs and propositions, and several approaches have been found successful.

One is to form a jointly funded consortium into which the taxpayer puts just enough money and effort to get things going, and insists on results that enable firms participating to "go it alone" from there onward.

Another is to run a continuing competition for limited government funds from bids made by individual firms with university partners; someone offering to go ahead with a good project on a limited subsidy has a good position.

Another is public purchasing of suitable goods, *e.g.,* chips for microcomputers to be used in schools.

Over the whole area, there needs to be a variety of financing methods, partly regulated by the market, but partly by agreed priorities.

Creating the Right Agencies: Politics

- Technology parks near campus (O,S);
- Generic technology centers or research associations (S,C);
- Corporate associates programs (O,C,S);
- Involvement of universities in schemes to spread awareness and consultancy (C,S); and
- Umbrella organizations like Massachusetts High Technology Council (O,C,S).

Behind everything that has been said is a need for confidence without feather-bedding. Without some timetable pressure, work can go on for too long before completion or cancellation. With too much time pressure, the longer term work gets squeezed out, and brilliant unorthodoxy is denied adequate opportunity. It is damaging, in particular, if support for the right mix is intermittently severely eroded or even withdrawn. Cancellation can be quick, but rebuilding is slow, so that a stop-go procedure, over several cycles, is inherently expensive.

The following check list of useful agencies is incomplete but may be useful:

- Technology parks on university campuses (These are very well-known, and rents can be graded so as to help the newcomers. Technology transfer is a key benefit, and help is cheap and at hand. University people learn about business and problem-solving.);
- Generic technology centers (These take in problems, send out missionaries, and act in a businesslike way. They should generate most of their funds, when mature. They can be in, adjacent to, or near universities.);
- Corporate associates programs — such as that of MIT (They are subscription schemes often selling "assistance vouchers."); and
- Awareness and consultancy schemes for new technologies (These employ teachers on short courses, of one day upwards, and university and other consultants to help follow up the courses.).

Appendix A
List of Conference Panels

Electronics

Panel Chairman:	Michiyuki Uenohara
Panel Speaker:	Björn Svedberg
Panel Members:	Pierre Aigrain, Lars Erik Björklund, Eric Bloch, Ingrid Bruce, George Bugliarello, Carl Erik Carlson, Sven Caspersen, Peter T. Davies, William R. Dill, Carmela S. Haklisch, Nico Hazewindus, Martti M. Kaila, Ewald Konecny, Rolf Lenschow, Finn Lied, V. Ludviksson, Mario di Lullo, Torsten Lundgren, José Mendes-Mourão, E. Mooser, Sam Nilsson, Sogo Okamura, Sven Olving, Toril Railo, Pekka Rautala, Hans Skoie, Lennart Stenberg, Michiaki Takaishi
Rapporteur:	Nils Starfelt

Pharmaceuticals

Panel Chairman:	Ernst Vischer
Panel Speaker:	Paolo Fasella
Panel Members:	H.B.G. Casimir, Georges Ferné, Michael Gibbons, Hans-Erik Hansen, Helmar Krupp, Carlos E. Kruytbosch, C.A. Ladage, Hans Landberg, Gudmund Larsson, Colm Ó hEocha, Lois S. Peters, Roger Svensson, Hugo Thiemann
Rapporteur:	Gerhard Miksche

Petroleum

Panel Chairman:	Moshe J. Lubin
Panel Speaker:	Francis Garnier
Panel Members:	H.L. Beckers, Duncan Davies, Martin Fehrm, David Gottlieb, Toralf Hernes, Einar Hope, Peter Lawætz, John Lundstøl, Johannes Moe
Rapporteur:	K. Gillis Een

Chemicals

Panel Chairman:	Fritz Fetting
Panel Speaker:	J. Robert Lovett
Panel Members:	Herbert I. Fusfeld, Sakari Kurronen, Ole H. Lie, Niilo Lou-

169

namaa, Valentin von Massow, Keichi Oshima, Kjell Sjöberg, Flemming Woldbye

Rapporteur: Agneta Boström

Mechanical Engineering

Panel Chairman: Jørgen Fakstorp
Panel Speaker: S.A.V. Swanson
Panel Members: Sven-Erik Andersson, Johannes Brotherus, G.L. Cooper, Guy Denielou, Björn Englund, Georges-A. Grin, G.R. Higginson, Alun Jones, Matti Kaario, Lucian A. Kasprzak, Börje Löfblad, Christel Nilsson, John Pick, Karl Steinhöfler, Dennys Watson
Rapporteur: Lennart Rohlin

Development of Competence in a World of Rapid Technical Change

Panel Chairman: G.R. Higginson
Panel Speaker: Erich Bloch
Panel Members: Lars Erik Björklund, K.F. Blomeyer, George Bugliarello, Michael Gibbons, Carmela S. Haklisch, Gudrun Hallgrimsdottir, Toralf Hernes, Einar Hope, Matti Kaario, Lucian A. Kasprzak, Ewald Konecny, Hans Landberg, Rolf Lenschow, José Mendes-Mourão, Gerhard Miksche, E. Mooser, Sam Nilsson, Toril Railo, Pekka Rautala, Kjell Sjöberg, Michiyuki Uenohara
Rapporteur: Torsten Lundgren

Functions of Research Institutes

Panel Chairman: Helmar Krupp
Panel Speaker: Johannes Moe
Panel Members: Ingrid Bruce, G.L. Cooper, Martin Fehrm, Herbert I. Fusfeld, Alun Jones, Martti M. Kaila, V. Ludviksson, John Lundstøl, Björn Nilsson, John Pick, Hans Skoie
Rapporteur: Björn Englund

Role of Universities in Economic Development – National, Regional, and International

Panel Chairman: Robert Chabbal
Panel Speaker: Valentin von Massow
Panel Members: H.L. Beckers, Sven Caspersen, Peter T. Davies, Francis Garnier, Sakari Kurronen, Gudmund Larsson, Markku Linna, Mario di Lullo, Christel Nilsson, Colm Ó hEocha, Sogo Okamura, Lois S. Peters, Michiaki Takaishi, Flemming Woldbye .

Rapporteur: Lena-Kajsa Sidén

Industrial Use of Technical Competence in Strategic Business Planning

Panel Chairman: Pierre Aigrain
Panel Speaker: William R. Dill
Panel Members: Sven-Erik Andersson, Johannes Brotherus, Jan Olof Carlsson, Duncan Davies, Jørgen Fakstorp, Nico Hazewindus, Carlos E. Kruytbosch, Ole H. Lie, Finn Lied, Börje Löfblad, Niilo Lounamaa, J. Robert Lovett, Sven Olving, Dennys Watson
Rapporteur: Gunnar Blockmar

Compatibility of University Integrity with Industrial Cooperation

Panel Chairman: Hugo Thiemann
Panel Speaker: Keichi Oshima
Panel Members: Carl Erik Carlson, H.B.G. Casimir, Guy Denielou, Georges-A. Grin, C.A. Ladage, Peter Lawætz, Karl Steinhöfler, S.A.V. Swanson, Robert D. Varrin, Ernst Vischer, Hanns P. Weisbarth
Rapporteur: Lennart Stenberg

Appendix B
List of Conference Participants

Conference on University–Industry Research Interactions
March 7–8, 1983
Stockholm, Sweden

Pierre Aigrain
Scientific Adviser to the President
Thomson
France

Sven-Erik Andersson
Managing Director
Swedish Institute of Production
  Engineering Research
Sweden

H.L. Beckers
Group Research Coordinator
Shell International
The Netherlands

Lars Erik Björklund
Scientific Attaché
Embassy of Finland
Sweden

Erich Bloch
Vice President
Technical Personnel Development
IBM
United States

Gunnar Blockmar
Civil Engineer
Royal Swedish Academy of
  Engineering Sciences (IVA)
Sweden

K.F. Blomeyer
Manager of Scientific Liaison Europe
Procter & Gamble
Belgium

Agneta Boström
National Swedish Board for
  Technical Development (STU)
Sweden

Gunnar Brodin
President
Royal Institute of Technology
Sweden

Johannes Brotherus
Director
Oy Wärtsilä Ab
Finland

Ingrid Bruce
Swedish Association of Graduate
  Engineers
Sweden

George Bugliarello
President
Polytechnic Institute of New York
United States

Carl Erik Carlson
Commissioner
The Finnish National Fund for
  Research and Development
Finland

Ingvar Carlsson
Deputy Prime Minister
Sweden

Jan Olof Carlsson
Deputy Director General
National Swedish Board for Technical
  Development (STU)
Sweden

H.B.G. Casimir
Senior Technical Officer (retired)
N.V. Philips Company
The Netherlands

Sven Caspersen
Rector
Aalborg University
Denmark

Robert Chabbal
President
Science and Technology Mission
Ministry for Research and Industry
France

G.L. Cooper
Science and Engineering Research
  Council (SERC)
Great Britain

Duncan Davies
Chairman
BCRA, Ltd.
Great Britain

Peter T. Davies
Government Adviser
Central Policy Review Staff

Cabinet Office
Great Britain

Guy Denielou
President
University of Technology at
  Compiègne
France

Harold A. Dewhurst
Director, Scientific Affairs
Owens-Corning Fiberglas
United States

William R. Dill
President
Babson College
United States

K. Gillis Een
Counsellor, Technical and Scientific
Swedish Embassy
Great Britain

Lennart Elg
Senior Executive Officer
Innovation Studies
National Swedish Board for
  Technical Development (STU)
Sweden

Björn Englund
Head of Section
National Swedish Board for
  Technical Development (STU)
Sweden

Jørgen Fakstorp
Vice President (retired)
F.L. Smidth & Co., A/S
Denmark

Paolo Fasella
Director General for Science,
  Research and Development
Commission of the European
  Communities

Martin Fehrm
Trygghetsrådet SAF-PTK
Sweden

Georges Ferné
Head of Section
University Research Policies
OECD

Fritz Fetting
Professor
Institute of Chemical Technology
Germany

Herbert I. Fusfeld
Director
Center for Science and Technology
  Policy
New York University
United States

Francis Garnier
Director
Solar Photochemistry Laboratory CNRS
France

Michael Gibbons
Head
Department of Liberal Studies in
  Science
University of Manchester
Great Britain

David Gottlieb
Special Assistant to the President
University of Houston System
United States

Georges-A. Grin
Science Advisor
Board of the Swiss Federal Institutes
  of Technology
Switzerland

Carmela S. Haklisch
Assistant Director

Center for Science and Technology
  Policy
New York University
United States

Folke Haldén
D. Econ
National University Board
Swedish Employers Confederation
  (SAF)
Sweden

Gudrun Hallgrimsdottir
Chief of Section
Ministry of Industry
Iceland

Gunnar Hambraeus
Chairman
Royal Swedish Academy of
  Engineering Sciences (IVA)
Sweden

Hans-Erik Hansen
Director
Federation of Danish Industries
Denmark

Nico Hazewindus
Director
Product Development
Philips International B. V.
The Netherlands

Toralf Hernes
Director
Royal Norwegian Council for
  Scientific and Industrial Research
Norway

G.R. Higginson
Professor
Department of Engineering
University of Durham
Great Britain

Einar Hope
Research Director
Center for Applied Research
Norwegian School of Economics and
 Business Administration
Norway

P. Ioakimidis
Economist, Managing Director
Renolit Hellas A.G.
Greece

Alun Jones
Assistant Director
The Technical Change Centre
Great Britain

Matti Kaario
Executive Director
The Engineering Society in
 Finland STS
Finland

Martti M. Kaila
Professor
Helsinki University of Technology
Finland

Lucian A. Kasprzak
Technical Assistant to Vice President
 of Technical Personnel Development
IBM
United States

Roland Kiessling
President
Sveriges Mekanförbund
Sweden

Ewald Konecny
Head of Research, Development, and
 Engineering Department
Drägerwerk AG
Germany

Helmar Krupp
Director

Institute for Systems Analysis and
 Innovation Research
Germany

Carlos E. Kruytbosch
Staff Associate
Office of Planning and Policy
 Analysis
National Science Foundation
United States

Sakari Kurronen
Dean
University of Oulu
Finland

C.A. Ladage
Ministry of Education and Science
The Netherlands

Hans Landberg
Secretary General
Swedish Council for Planning and
 Coordination of Research (FRN)
Sweden

Gudmund Larsson
Landsorganisationen
Sweden

Peter Lawaetz
Rector
Technical University of Denmark
Denmark

Rolf Lenschow
Professor
The Norwegian Institute of
 Technology
Norway

Ole H. Lie
Senior Vice President
Technology and Research
Norsk Hydro a.s.
Norway

Finn Lied
Director
Statoil
Norway

Markku Linna
Director
Department for Higher Education and
 Research
Ministry of Education
Finland

Börje Löfblad
Director
Sandvik AB
Sweden

Niilo Lounamaa
Director of Development
Kemira Oy
Finland

J. Robert Lovett
President and Member, Board of
 Directors
Air Products Europe, Inc.
Great Britain

Moshe J. Lubin
Vice President
Research & Development and
 Patent & License
The Standard Oil Company (Ohio)
United States

V. Ludviksson
The National Research Council
Iceland

Mario di Lullo
Director
DJ Programme
NATO

Torsten Lundgren
Swedish Employers' Confederation

(SA)
Sweden

John Lundstøl
Consultant
Central Committee for Norwegian
 Research
Norway

Valentin von Massow
Head
Science Policy and Promotion of
 Research Division
Federal Ministry of Education and
 Science
Germany

José Mendes-Mourão
President
National Board for Scientific and
 Technological Research
Portugal

Gerhard Miksche
National Swedish Board for
 Technical Development (STU)
Sweden

Johannes Moe
Managing Director
Foundation for Scientific and
 Industrial Research
Norwegian Institute of Technology
 (SINTEF)
Norway

E. Mooser
Vice President
Swiss National Science Foundation
Switzerland

Curt Nicolin
Chairman
ASEA AB
Sweden

Björn Nilsson
V. Chairman of the Board
Philips Elektronikindustrier AB
Svenska Philipsföretagen AB
Sweden

Christel Nilsson
Educational Relations
AB Volvo
Sweden

Sam Nilsson
Director
The International Federation of
  Institutes for Advanced Study
  (IFIAS)
Sweden

Colm Ó hEocha
President
University College, Galway
Ireland

Sogo Okamura
Director General
Japan Society for the Promotion of
  Science
Japan

Sven Olving
Professor
Chalmers University of Technology
Sweden

Keichi Oshima
President
Industrial Research Institute, Japan
Japan

Lois S. Peters
Senior Research Associate
Center for Science and Technology
  Policy
New York University
United States

John Pick
Professor of Materials Technology
  (ret.)
University of Aston
Great Britain

Toril Railo
Executive Officer
Royal Ministry of Industry
Norway

Pekka Rautala
Professor
Outokumpu Oy
Finland

Lennart Rohlin
Science and Technology Counselor
Swedish Embassy
France

Ingvar Seregard
President
Federation of Salaries Employees in
  Industry and Services (PTK)
Sweden

Lena-Kajsa Sidén
Head of International Activities
Royal Swedish Academy of
  Engineering Sciences (IVA)
Sweden

Thomas Sidenbladh
Deputy Undersecretary
Ministry of Industry
Sweden

Kjell Sjöberg
Professor
Royal Institute of Technology
Sweden

Hans Skoie
Research Director
Institute for Studies in Research

and Higher Education
Norway

Nils G. Starfelt
Counselor, Science and Technology
Swedish Embassy
United States

Elias M. Stassinopoulos
Vice-Chairman and General Manager
The M.S. Stassinopoulos Group
Greece

Karl Steinhöfler
Federal Chamber of Commerce
Austria

Lennart Stenberg
Senior Planning Officer
National Swedish Board for Technical
  Development (STU)
Sweden

Björn Svedberg
President and Chief Executive Officer
L.M. Ericsson Telephone Company
Sweden

Roger Svensson
Executive Research Secretary
Swedish Council for Planning and
  Coordination of Research (FRN)
Sweden

S.A.V. Swanson
Pro Rector
Imperial College
Great Britain

Michiaki Takaishi
First Secretary in Education
Japanese Delegation to the OECD

Hugo Thiemann
Member of the Board
Swiss Academy of Engineering
  Sciences
Switzerland

Michiyuki Uenohara
Executive Vice President and
  Director, Research
NEC Corporation
Japan

Hans Ursing
Managing Director
Trygghetsrådet SAF-PTK
Sweden

Robert D. Varrin
University Coordinator for Research
University of Delaware
United States

Ernst Vischer
Vice Chairman, Board of Directors
Ciba-Geigy
Switzerland

Dennys Watson
Head of Task Force for Innovation
  Coordination
Commission of the European
  Communities

Hanns P. Weisbarth
Vice President, Engineering
BMW of North America, Inc.
United States

Flemming Woldbye
Director
The Danish Research Administration
Denmark

Index

182

Index

need for, 151–154
strengthening cooperation, 161–167
"University/Industry Research
    Relationships—Myths, Realities, and
    Potentials,", 1
US Council for Chemical Research,
    (CCR), 51–57, 59
US Court of Appeals, 21–22
US Industrial Research Institute (IRI), 2
US Steel, 145
US University–Industry Connections, 1

Vischer, Ernst, 4
VLSI, 26

Vocational Exhibition, 130
von Massow, Valentin, 5, 113

Wage-earner funds, 156
Weber, Ernst, 19
West Germany. *See* Germany, Federal
    Republic of
Westinghouse, 126
Wharton Econometric Model, 122
Work force, US, 74
World Bank, 110
Wright Brothers, 143, 147
WSI, 99

Xerox Corporation, 123